EMPOWER

YOUR

CONTROL WORRY AND ANXIETY, DEVELOP A POSITIVE MENTAL ATTITUDE, AND MASTER YOUR MINDSET

THOUGHTS

SCOTT ALLAN

Empower Your
Thoughts

*Control Worry and Anxiety, Develop a Positive Mental
Attitude, and Master Your Mindset*

More Bestselling Titles From Scott Allan

Empower Your Thoughts

Drive Your Destiny

Relaunch Your Life

The Discipline of Masters

Do the Hard Things First

Undefeated

No Punches Pulled

Fail Big

Built for Stealth

Check out the complete collection of books and training here:

www.scottallanbooks.com

Empower Your
Thoughts

*Control Worry and Anxiety, Develop a Positive Mental
Attitude, and Master Your Mindset*

By Scott Allan

Scott Allan PUBLISHING
MASTER YOUR LIFE ONE BOOK AT A TIME

www.scottallanbooks.com

CONTENTS

"Man is made or unmade by himself; in the armory of thought he forges the weapons by which he destroys himself; he also fashions the tools with which he builds for himself heavenly mansions of joy and strength and peace. By the right choice and true application of thought, man ascends to the Divine Perfection; by the abuse and wrong application of thought, he descends below the level of the beast. Between these two extremes are all the grades of character, and man is their maker and master."

— **James Allen**,
author of *As a Man Thinketh*

Empower Your Thoughts:
An Overview

> *"People tend to dwell more on negative things than on good things. So, the mind then becomes obsessed with negative things, with judgments, guilt and anxiety produced by thoughts about the future and so on."*
>
> — **Eckhart Tolle**, Bestselling author of
> *The Power of Now*

Do you want more control over your creative thoughts? Are you held back by a mind that is stuck in the negative past instead of focused on a compelling future? Are thoughts of fear and worry causing you stress and anxiety?

When your thoughts are given a free pass to act without restraint, your mind becomes a machine set to autopilot. You become immersed in anxiety and worry that lead to fear-based decisions and inaction. Your thoughts, if allowed to take over your mind unhinged, could sabotage future opportunity and rob you of positive experiences you should be enjoying.

If you are like most people, your head is at war with itself when your mind is concerned. Thoughts run on, seemingly without purpose or restraint. It is as if someone turns up the dial in your head when you have a bad day, a conflict with someone, or when everything is going against you.

At these times, it feels as if you are a slave to the master in your own mind. You are the master of your mind. It is this inner dialogue that rambles on, full of self-criticisms and put-downs. It is the noise within that makes us want to scream for it to stop.

Our thoughts can either hold us back or push us forward. They can help us or hinder our progress. But the direction of your mind is up to you.

You cannot manage and eliminate all the negative thoughts you have. Most of them are just passing through on the way to somewhere else. These are random thoughts about nothing, and we don't have to concern ourselves with them.

But constant and repetitive thoughts of anger, grudges, scarcity, greed, and worry are destructive to your overall mental health. Over time, "bad thinking" can break down the walls of your mental fortress. And if those walls fall, life can become like a bad ride.

In this book, *Empower Your Thoughts*, I will teach you the strategies and right mindset to master your thoughts, take greater control of your emotions, and manage your internal dialogue.

You are the warrior of your own mind. You will learn to harness this power and drive your thoughts, mental energy, and creative aspirations to build everything you've ever dreamed of.

I know what it is like to struggle with a mind that is "out-of-control". When your thoughts run free from restraint, they can take over your mind and drive you to *react* instead of taking intentional action. How often have you stopped yourself and said, "Why did I think like that?" or "What was I thinking?" It appears we are at the mercy of an entity that is out-of-control.

> *"Overwhelm is, most often, a mindset. If you think about all the things you have to do, you'll be face down on the floor. It really helps to break it down into smaller pieces."*

— **Jen Sincero**, bestselling author of
You Are a Badass

My goal with *Empower Your Thoughts* is to give you back the power to think freely again, to express ideas without restraint, and to explore the freedom of creativity—the greatest freedom there is.

The biggest prison that exists is not housed with deadly criminals, but it is the prison of our own minds. Your thoughts are the gatekeepers, and negative, pessimistic thinking is the crime. It is time to let your thoughts free and explore the undiscovered creativity and freedom hiding behind negative thought patterns.

We spend too much effort on majoring in minor things. The people who work on changing their lives, making a difference, and adding value to the lives of others, are committed to doing the work that most people won't. They are engaged in activities that drive momentum and make the most out of their limited time each day.

While the millions are engaged in television every day (the world's biggest destroyer of creativity and lost time suck), the few are working toward a goal, a dream, and a purpose that can change their lives, and the lives of those around them.

This book is about harnessing your thoughts in a way that empowers your mind to develop a strong thinking mindset and positive attitude.

A mindset is more than just a "way of thinking"; it is a way of being. You must be persistent in your pursuits as you act every day toward fulfilling your dreams.

Creating and maintaining a positive mindset—and the accompanying attitude—is the key element. Instead of just "being positive" because that is what you are told successful people are, you are going to discover the reason for being positive.

Many people don't know what to focus on, so they are focused on everything, and as a result, accomplish little. In today's world, that has never been easier to do with all our gadgets, bells and whistles, and shiny objects competing for attention.

At every turn we are being encouraged to join the latest website, play the newest game, watch the latest TV show, or download the newest app. Your thoughts have a lot of competition!

But, none of that matters. A mind that is trained to stay focused isn't in competition with anything or anyone. You don't have to purposefully ignore the distractions because you are not compelled to feed into it.

You can ignore 90 percent of what doesn't matter and focus on the 10 percent that does. Instead of feeling like you have to be engaged in everything going on around you, we are going to talk about "focused choices," where you selectively choose the thoughts you want to have, work toward empowering these thoughts with a positive mindset that rocks, and finally, channeling all of this into shaping your ideas to forge the future you desire.

It is a simple formula: Know what you want. Empower and train your thoughts to focus on this desire. Forge an attitude that supports your purpose. Drive everything toward taking intentional action toward your creative ideas.

Throughout this book are many tips, strategies, and activities for you to implement as you read. You will learn how to apply the power of positive, confident, creative thought to get whatever it is you truly desire the most.

Let's start the journey.

Turn to the next page and start reading...

Empower Your Thoughts.

"You can never become a great man or woman until you have overcome anxiety, worry, and fear. It is impossible for an anxious person, a worried one, or a fearful one to perceive truth; all things are distorted and thrown out of their proper relations by such mental states, and those who are in them cannot read the thoughts of God."

— Wallace D. Wattles,
author of *The Science of Getting Rich*

PART I

Empower Your Thoughts

Chapter 1

Four Life Lessons My Father Taught Me About Empowering Thought

"You have powers you never dreamed of. You can do things you never thought you could do. There are no limitations in what you can do except the limitations of your own mind."

— Darwin P. Kingsley

When I was a kid, my father taught me four unforgettable lessons about the importance of empowering your thoughts. Throughout my life, I would carry these lessons with me and implement them whenever the situation called for it.

My father did a lot of reading, mostly self-help books that focused on personal development. He was always committed to making a better life for himself and his family. He would share these ideas with me when I looked troubled, or struggling with some internal demon I didn't understand.

When he gave me advice, he would tell me to look for the solution to every problem by thinking it through and analyzing all the possibilities. He would often say, "The biggest problem with people is that they don't think enough."

Many of the lessons I learned in those days were picked up from reading the classic self-help books: *As a Man Thinketh* by James Allen,

The Power of Positive Thinking by Norman Vincent Peale, and *How to Stop Worrying and Start Living* by Dale Carnegie.

There were many powerful lessons my father shared with me over the years that shaped both my thinking and mindset for the life I was born to lead years later. I'm going to share four of those lessons with you here. Embrace these lessons and apply them to your own mindset so that you can master your own thoughts.

Lesson One: Train Your Mind to Think

My father once said to me, "You should learn to think for yourself so that others don't have to do the thinking for you."

I didn't understand the principle at the time, but over the years, the lesson made sense as I trained my mind to ask deeper questions about the important matters of life. By thinking for myself, I was able to make higher-level choices about my life.

I realized that I could choose to question things such as logic and reality. I could formulate my own ideas instead of relying on the wisdom and ideas of others to do this for me. In other words, by thinking *for* myself, I could have more freedom to *be* myself.

Here are some questions for you: What motivates you? Why do you believe what you believe? Are your thoughts your own or someone else's thoughts and opinions? What do you think about when you are alone? What thoughts make you feel passionate about living the life you have?

By tapping into your thoughts with deeper questions, you open up the capacity to make better choices. You don't have to accept everything as it is just because someone once said it is a certain way.

When you think for yourself, you are deciding to take control over your own mind. Allow others to think for you, and you are allowing them to control your mind.

This isn't to say we shouldn't ask for help, but when you are faced with a situation that requires you to figure out the next step, take the time to think the problem through. You should form your own opinions about things only after you've spent time analyzing, questioning, and building your own logical conclusions.

By consistently learning and training your mind to think more deeply, you can trust and depend more on your own thoughts and ideas. Over time, practicing this lesson helps build strength of character, and problem solving becomes a more natural learning path.

Take the First Initiative

While other people would stand around waiting for someone to tell them what to do, I learned to take the initiative and act first. By thinking for myself, people would come to me for the answers to problems they struggled with. In this case, I would always challenge the person first by asking questions: "Well, what is the problem? What would you do if you had five minutes to figure out a solution, and nobody else was around?"

I learned that you can motivate others to think for themselves and create leaders out of these people. Not everyone will follow this path, and the people who would rather have others think for them end up strapped to work they don't like because they refuse to change. Thought changes you, and it can change others, too.

By putting your thoughts into action, and showing others how to do the same, you can form a powerful alliance with a group of people focused toward a specific goal. Everyone can think for himself or herself. They may think differently, but their combined efforts and creative ideas have the power to shape the future.

There is a worldwide demand for people who can raise their thoughts to a higher level. People will pay you for your ability to empower their workers to become more efficient or to show them better ways to run their company more productively.

Do you want to empower your thoughts and learn to control the way you think and behave? Or, would you rather work for someone else who does the thinking for you? You can choose your own path in life; there is no right or wrong direction if you end up where you want to be.

You can discipline your thoughts to direct your life in any way you want. In doing so, you become the greatest contributor to a life of creativity and diversity.

Lesson Two: Remove Fearful Thoughts with Gratitude

My father told me that you should observe the thoughts you have about fear. Fearful thoughts are inevitable, and the greatest challenge for most people is what to do when fearful thoughts take over.

He said: "Everyone is afraid, and people handle it in different ways. Some people listen to their fearful thinking and do foolish things. Other people listen to their thoughts while observing the fear that grows there, and they figure out an approach to turn it into empowerment."

He also said that fearful thoughts will either push you to act so that you are no longer afraid. But thoughts full of fear will force you to retreat. Once you make the decision to run away from fear, this becomes your new default behavior for handling difficult situations. Face what you fear, and continue to do that, until it becomes your new habit.

Don't run away from fear and allow fearful thinking to steal your opportunity to live your life and go after what you want. People who aspire to greatness arrive there by taking on the challenges they fear most, and crushing their fear-based mindset.

Everyone has a choice in how they react to fearful thoughts. You can either live in fear of fear, experiencing it as a sense of impending doom, or you can push back against the thoughts that create your fear.

Controlling my fear was the second lesson in empowering my thoughts. I started to notice the areas of my life where fear was at its greatest: finances, the fear of failure, self-doubt, and uncertainty. My thoughts were rife with fear, but they had become so ingrained as part of my psyche, I hadn't taken notice that they were there.

Identifying the thoughts that I had associated with certain situations provided me with the clarity to seize these thoughts, instead of letting them run wild. For example, when I had thoughts of scarcity, I would be fearful of losing money, and worried about never having enough. If I was doing public speaking, my head would fill with the dread of failure and being judged by the audience. It was as though a war were happening inside my head, and all I could do was watch it happen.

Thoughts Full of Fear Affect Us in Many Ways

If much of your thinking is fear-based, your default actions will be based on your fears. For instance, if you fear having no money, you might react by hoarding and skimping. But this reinforces the fear of having no money. By denying that you are giving into fearful thoughts, you give them more power to take over.

Fearful thoughts create "scarcity" thinking. You believe that you never have enough, no matter how much is gained. If your focus is always fixated on the things you don't have, you spend your mental energy focused on what is missing in your life. You're always in pursuit of the next best thing. Then, when you finally get it, you want the next best thing after that.

This creates an obsession to keep accumulating stuff that fills up your life but still leaves you empty. You constantly want more of the things your mind desires. It becomes a bottomless pit that can never be filled.

Scarcity thinking is a breeding ground for fear: the fear of loss, the fear of living in poverty, and the fear of not having enough.

It's a double-edged sword: the more you get, the more you want. Scarcity thinking becomes a bad habit that you continue to return to whenever a situation arises that threatens your security. It turns into an endless loop that is never fulfilled.

This all changed when I recognized the fearful thoughts as they appeared. It was old fear that I had never dealt with. In seeing it for the first time, I could replace this bad thinking with new thoughts. You can do the same thing.

Instead of thinking, "They're going to laugh at me," I would think, "These people are going to love my speech." Instead of thinking "I wish I had more money," I would replace this with, "I have all the money I need."

My father said you should always practice **gratitude**. Love what you have and let go of what you don't. Nothing should be taken for granted he said, not even the air we breathe or the water so easily accessible in our homes.

Be grateful for what you have today and don't get caught up in worrisome thoughts of the future. When we focus on the uncertainty of the future, our thoughts leave the present moment, and this opens pathways for more fear to take over.

Gratitude and fearful thoughts cannot exist in the same space. You can choose how you want to share that space in your head.

Gratitude Is in the Now

You can replace scarcity thinking with gratitude. It is the only cure I know of that works. If you have $100 in your account, be grateful that it's not $10. If you have $10, be grateful you don't owe $10. In every situation, look for the opportunity to express gratitude and turn your fears of scarcity into thoughts that focus on thriving.

Tell the people in your life that you feel lucky because they are in your life. Expressing your gratitude toward the people you care about is the best solution to keeping fear away. Nobody is fearful when they are appreciative of the people that they share their lives with.

But there is another challenge. We should have gratitude for the people who cause us suffering as well; they are teaching us something valuable about ourselves.

Don't lose another moment fixated on people you resent or cause you mental grief. In the end, your mind will form the model of what you focus on. When you fix your thoughts on what you love, you feel great. Focus on things you hate, and your attitude adopts the thoughts that feed into this hatred.

When we have conflict, in most cases we think it is because of the other person. But the conflict is inside. The other people just set it off and we react to it out of old conditioning. People that bring stress and fear in relationships can also be good teachers.

Many of the people whom I always said that I "didn't like" showed me my lack of tolerance, lack of kindness, and how much fear I was holding onto.

By recognizing the lessons behind the fear, I could change my thinking and see the situations I disliked as necessary learning curves.

"Our subconscious minds have no sense of humor, play no jokes and cannot tell the difference between reality and an imagined thought or image. What we continually think about eventually will manifest in our lives."

— Sidney Madwed

Lesson Three: Expand Beyond Your Comfort Zone

My father once told me, "The reason people struggle to change is because they don't challenge the thoughts they have, and prefer to stay stuck in the comfort of their own minds. You should challenge your comfort zone of fear and do something different every day."

As the late bestselling author Susan Jeffers once said, "You can feel the fear and do it anyway."

No matter what fears you have, they don't have to control you. Don't give them permission to do that. When you feel the fear, step back and observe what it is you are afraid of. What thoughts are you having that are creating your fear? When you move against the thoughts causing you to feel fearful, they vanish and lose that power over you. Taking direct action is the only cure I know of.

According to statistics, 83% of people want to write a book, and only 1% ever do. If this is your goal, start by writing a brief outline. Jot down some words on paper related to your topic. Then, write one page. If you can't do this, write down a sentence. Sometimes, you need to break your fear down into mini-steps that work.

Write down the actions you could take and choose one action. **Do something.** If you don't, your thoughts will lock into a rotating spin, and you'll keep reliving the same fears, day after day. I know many people have spent their lives regretting all the things they never did. In the end, you'll regret living in fear and not doing what you were born to do.

It is perfectly okay to try and <u>fail</u> the first time. You won't always succeed on the first attempt, but putting your best efforts forward will reduce the fear and make each action easier to take. Those who manage their fears, and do something to push forward, always persevere over those who hide and don't confront the thoughts keeping them stuck.

I always experience fear if I think about trying something new that is out of my comfort zone. This can be an interview, launching a new book, or meeting someone for the first time. This fear is often attached to feelings of rejection, the fear of failure, or the fear of not measuring up to expectations.

The more fear you have, the better off you are. Fear is an indicator of what it is you should be doing. Use your fearful thoughts as learning gauges to measure what it is you need to work on. The more things you are afraid of, the more action you can take to start diminishing your fears.

It is a faulty belief that having fearful thoughts is a bad thing. It is your fear that prompts you to take further action—even when you are afraid. You will never be rid of it because every time you step out of your bubble, fear is waiting for you. Your fearful thoughts are signals that either you are doing something wrong, or you are putting off doing something that needs to be done.

Your fearful ego will avoid taking risks by doing mindless activities that keep you occupied. Turning on the TV, playing a video game for endless hours, or seeing what other people are doing on social media can mask your fear. Once these distractions end, you are back to feeling anxiety again.

Practice becoming self-observant of those moments when you are procrastinating or engaging in escapist activities. When you have the urge to run away, you are feeding into fearful thoughts that keep you stuck.

Most people stay within the safe confines of a mind that is afraid to push itself toward change and growth. When you try something different, you can feel the resistance inside your own head. Something is telling you this is not the usual protocol, and that you had better be careful or else you might...

FAIL.

The fear of failure affects more people than you know. But the real failure comes with not living up to your potential and staying small behind the shadows of what you could be. Nothing is wasted as much as the life of a person who wastes their mind. If you want to succeed, take a risk and do what scares you.

Some people live by the philosophy that if you jump out of a plane without a chute on, you'll figure out how to have a safe landing somehow. There are many people out there with perfectly good chutes that never make that jump.

Challenge your comfort zone. Jump out of it at least once a day. Push past that fear barrier a little more each day.

Remember the movie scene in *The Fellowship of the Ring* (*Lord of the Rings*), when Frodo and Sam set out on their journey from the Shire? Sam had stopped at the border of the Shire and said, "If I take one more step, I will have gone farther than I ever had before."

Go on. Take that step now.

Lesson Four: Be the Master of Your Circumstances

When I was growing up, I had a lot of anxiety about my life. I worried about everything, and allowed external situations to bring me down. I performed poorly in academics at school so I was convinced that I would be a failure in life, too.

I shared this internal fear and worry with my father one day. He then taught me the most important lesson for empowering my thoughts.

He said, "You can't choose the environment or circumstances that you are born into, but you can create the life you want by deciding what to do with those circumstances. This is so much bigger than believing that your life is a by-product of your education, upbringing and environment."

When you just sit back and allow life to become whatever it may be, circumstances will shape and mold your life according to the desires of other people. If you want to be free, set your own goals in life and draft a plan. Your thoughts will form a natural channel of continuity to ensure you get there.

If you have a clear direction as to where you are going, and can say, "Yes, this is what I want to have!" If you are willing to do anything to get it, then everything changes.

By making a firm decision to be the master of your environment, and by striving to break any obstacle that challenge your vision of who you want to be, you step up to a new level. You can make the choice not to settle.

Your thoughts—when nurtured—create the desirable situations and quality of life that you want. If your thoughts are neglected and you let things happen by default, you'll end up in a situation doing the things you hate. You'll be working hard to build someone else's dream instead of your own.

One of the reasons people fail to live the life they want is they end up believing they have no control over their lives. They are stuck in the same job year after year, in the same crappy relationships, living a life that they come to regret. They make excuses that stick, instead of creating new habits that stick in order to change their behavior.

You are not a product of your environment or circumstances. You have been influenced by these things, but not molded from them.

"The Queen of All Media"

Oprah Winfrey, dubbed the "Queen of All Media" and ranked the richest African American of the twentieth century, was born into poverty in rural Mississippi to a teenage single mother. Oprah spent the first six years of her young life with her grandmother, who at the time was so poor, Oprah had to wear potato sacks for dresses.

"I don't think of myself as a poor, deprived ghetto girl who made good. I think of myself as somebody who from an early age knew she was responsible for herself—and I had to make good."

— Oprah Winfrey

But Oprah decided at a young age that she didn't want to live in poverty. She refused to let her current situation define what she could become. Oprah defeated adversity and defied a life of hardship and poverty to become America's most influential talk-show host, and the "most influential woman in the world".

The Master of Circumstance

You can master your circumstances. Regardless of what difficulties you are facing, or the size of the mountain you must climb to get to your goal, you can only be defeated by your own thoughts.

This isn't to say that you are solely responsible for the environment you are born into. People born into poverty, violence, or "temporary limitations" in various forms didn't choose this way of life. But, if you come to realize that you can choose your thoughts, you gain total control over the direction of your life.

This is the definition of genuine power: When you no longer blame external circumstances for your present life condition. You can fully accept responsibility for where you are at right now and acknowledge that you are the only one can change it if you don't like it.

So, what are the circumstances that you need to feel fulfilled? What would you have to change about yourself in order to bring that positive element into your life? What can you do today that you have never done before that would have a major impact on the way you live your life and enjoy every day?

Focus on getting in touch with what really drives you, and what makes you tick. Developing a good attitude begins with taking responsibility for your life. It is about deciding on and making the hardline choices between what you'll accept and reject, instead of just taking whatever is handed to you.

Key Takeaway

Lesson One: Always think for yourself. Develop the habit of questioning everything.

Lesson Two: Always keep gratitude at the forefront of your mind. Make a gratitude list every morning of three things you are grateful for. When you feel yourself slipping into fearful thoughts and being led astray, bring your mind back to the present moment.

Lesson Three: Escaping from yourself is a reaction to fearful thoughts. This creates stress and can cause some big anxiety issues. We can cope with this by taking direct action against our fears. Break out of your comfort zone. No matter the fear; it doesn't control you. Let your actions guide the fear to do what you want.

Lesson Four: We are not slaves to our circumstances, but masters of them. Your thoughts can defeat or elevate you here. In believing you can gain control over the course of your life by directing your thoughts, you are able to take responsibility for your life.

Chapter 2

Guiding Thought and Empowering Mindfulness

> *"Remember, happiness doesn't depend upon who you are or what you have; it depends solely upon what you think."*
>
> — **Dale Carnegie,** Author of
> *How to Win Friends and Influence People*

A powerful form of harnessing your thoughts is practiced through a discipline known as **mindfulness**.

Mindfulness has been practiced for centuries by masters of the mind to gain greater clarity and awareness over the thoughts being created in the present moment. Without a handle on what we are thinking, we fall victim to *Monkey Mind*, where our thoughts run rampant and become reactive. This leads to all sorts of problems: anxiety, worry, and compulsive negative thinking.

Your thoughts can serve you in two ways. In one way, they bring peace of mind, joy, and happiness into your life. This is the result of how you feel when you're thinking clearly with thoughts of love, gratitude, creativity, and clarity. You feel good and your perception of the world is positive.

The other way is an invitation to thoughts of anger, frustration, irritability, or confusion. Something is not right in your life, and you think about this one thing constantly until it becomes all you have. It could be an unresolved issue or someone that is causing you grief. But the question is: *Are you giving away your power? Are you letting your thoughts run the show? Is your thinking influencing how you feel?*

It is normal and natural. We will always have thoughts running through our heads every day. The person who is committed to mastering their thoughts will be able to control their emotions at will. That, in my opinion, is true mental mastery.

So many people are focused on the externals to bring them what they want, and then they act disappointed when nothing goes right.

For example:

"Oh, I thought she liked me, but now, I feel rejected."

"Nobody is going to accept me. I feel like I am nothing."

"This wouldn't have happened if only...."

You can train your mind to sync with your thoughts. This is self-observation. You are aware of what you are thinking, but you aren't concerned with doing anything about it. Sometimes we can't. We must learn to be thinking above and beyond ourselves. By raising your mind to a state of mindfulness, your perception begins to change. When you see everything differently, you think differently.

If you remain mindful of the thoughts that crop up and threaten to ruin your day, you will discover that, not only can you have greater control over what you are thinking, but can also reject any thought that doesn't comply with your present emotional state.

Let's say that today you decide to not express your anger. Perhaps you often have episodes where you just lose it or you tell yourself, "I can't take it anymore." But what you tell yourself becomes your thought, and this forms a reaction. If you think, "I'm going to lose it right now!" you probably will. You will look for a reason to lash out and, your thoughts will form into whatever emotion you are wanting to express.

This is definitely a bad day. Everything is going to pieces. In this case, your thoughts and emotions will begin a train of thinking in direct relation to the experiences you are having. You might overexaggerate your negative experience by making it out to be worse than it is. The world is coming apart. Everyone hates you. Even dogs won't come near you.

Negative thinking doesn't just happen without your permission. This is an important lesson to learn. You give yourself permission to think, feel, and react. You can choose to view your life as a train wreck or a nice ride through the mountains.

How can mindfulness help you overcome the impulse to have negative thoughts? Most people fail at thinking before they fail at anything else. As you will learn, mastering your thoughts is difficult. Like anything that requires change, you have to develop the habit of focusing on your thoughts as they are happening. This doesn't mean you have to think about every thought you have, but rather, be conscious of the thoughts negatively impacting your state of mind.

You can see the cup as half empty or half full. You can live in a relaxed state of being that mindfulness gives you, or, be out of control as your thoughts lead your mind down darker paths to greater suffering.

Mindfulness Techniques

Here are a few techniques to help you practice mindfulness in your day-to-day. Commit to healing your thoughts with mindfulness practice for a minimum of ten minutes a day.

Listen to deep relaxing music.

Music has many benefits that impact our health in positive ways. The kind of music you listen to influences your thoughts. Listening to the right kind of music can connect your thoughts to a deeper level of emotion and harmony, driving you to change your state immediately.

Here are three ways listening to meditation or relaxing music throughout your day greatly improves your quality of daily living:

Relaxing music improves quality of sleep: Studies have proven the impact of relaxing music and how it positively influences your sleep patterns. The consensus is, it relaxes your mind and improves the quality of your thoughts during sleep. Before bed, it is recommended you turn off the tv and shutdown your computer at least one hour before turning in. Block off the last 30 minutes for winding down with relaxing music.

Relaxing music is therapy for the brain. Relaxing music can act as therapy and pull you out of a depression as it helps the brain to form creative ideas. It improves concentration and can reduce anxiety, blood pressure, and pain as well as improve your mental alertness, mood and memory.

Relaxing music reduces stress. You should listen to relaxing music three times a day for a minimum of ten minutes each session. Stress levels can build throughout the day. You can manage this with deep relaxation music. The best part is, it helps to keep your thoughts in check.

Find a quiet place you can be alone for ten minutes and tune into your music. The song **Weightless by Marconi Union** is effective at calming your heartrate, slowing down breathing and stimulates brain activity

Practice Visual Imaging.

I discovered this form of wakeful meditation years ago. You have a powerhouse of an imagination. Are you using it? Do you imagine the future you could have? Can you visualize overcoming your difficulties to become better at who you are and what you can do?

Visualizing a positive event can be a powerful form of mind training. Where would your thoughts be if you only had good ones? What if you could catch the negative thoughts you don't want before they take hold?

Imagine what it would be like if you had a perfect day. How would you feel? Who are you with? What are you thinking and feeling? By imagining yourself as a free agent (meaning free from the suffering of bad thinking) you can mold your moments and hours into anything you like.

Crush Your Mental Monster.

I used to get headaches when I fell into a negative thought mind trap. This would happen often and then one day it occurred to me: negative thinking—criticism, comparing yourself to others, feeling dissatisfied with your place in life—is painful to live with.

When we voluntarily put ourselves down, it sinks our self-esteem and crushes our confidence. There are many ways to suffer but beating yourself up mentally is the most painful.

You don't have to believe the lies (and most of it is lies). The self-critical monster is only real in your head, but **it is real**. You can crush this monster with the strategies in this book. One strategy I would recommend to you is what I call the "Crush it Up" strategy. Here is how it works:

Imagine all the bad thoughts you are having, and the negative vices and people/places that are filling you up with anger. The reason they have power over you is because you are letting those thoughts run through your head.

Now, imagine gathering all this stuff and visualize yourself crushing it into a ball. Keep crushing everything down until it is the size of a baseball. Then, throw it into a fire. Watch it burn.

In your mind, picture starting with a new slate. Place a positive quote into your mind and hold it there. Repeat this quote to yourself. Think about nothing else. If other thoughts enter, let them pass though. You are the master of your own thoughts. You are the gatekeeper of what enters your mind. Nobody can mess with you. The voices of the past can't hurt you. Old failures have nothing on you. You are free.

Practice this exercise at the end of the day when you are tired, worn-out, or you need to reset your thinking for the next day.

Thought Conditioning and Triggers

Have you ever been around a person or in a situation that just made you feel negative? Did it affect your thoughts first, as you were pulled into your habit of overthinking the situation and beginning to defend yourself against it?

Two big triggers of bad thoughts are when people are overly critical of you, and when you are in a situation that challenge your fear. No matter what, you get sucked down the rabbit hole of "stinking-thinking".

By the end of the day you are anxious, fearful, and sick of the day you've had. But it doesn't have to be this way.

Here is what you can do. Using mindfulness—that is, being totally aware of your thoughts as they occur in real time—make a note of what triggers your thoughts to become fearful, worrisome, or anxious. Is it a person whom you have a conflict with? Is it a situation or a place you were in? We all have these situations in our lives. But to pinpoint the root issue, you have to know where it begins. What was the trigger?

Your thoughts are heavily attached to people, places, and things. Depending on the nature of the experience, you will have good thoughts that are positive, supportive, and healthy. You could also have negative thoughts that creates stress, fear, and anxiety.

To deal with the trigger, you must deal with the source. If it is a difficult relationship that causes your thinking to go dark, putting distance between yourself and that person would be one option to protect your state of mind. This could be a manager or co-worker, your ex-spouse, or a parent. If distance isn't possible, try healing affirmations when you are in the presence of this person. Carry these with you wherever you go.

Affirmations are statements grounded in positivity to help us develop better control over thinking. Instead of letting your thoughts turn to anger, resentment, or revenge, repeat your affirmations to yourself when in the presence of people who influence your state of mind.

Replacing Negative Thoughts to Win the Mental War

You will always struggle with negative thoughts. This is unavoidable. You are constantly challenged by people and events that directly influence your thought patterns. How you react to the situation sets the stage for the level of thinking you rise to in order to deal with it.

Your aim isn't to eliminate negative thoughts forever. This would be an unrealistic goal. But what you <u>can</u> do is arm yourself with new tools, tactics, and strategies. If you go to war, you'll need the right weapons for the fight. And there are many days when the only enemy is your own mind.

Thoughts of worry, doubt, depression, and fear are a part of our makeup. We may always be worried about something, but we can overcome worry by staying fixed in the present moment.

"What day is at?" asked Pooh. "It's today," squeaked Piglet. "My favorite day," said Pooh.

Most of our worries are focused on future events that may never happen. But our fearful thoughts are fixed on an imaginary outcome it thinks will someday arrive and ruin everything. Your thoughts could be focused in on financial ruin, a relationship ending, or fears about getting ill.

Here is a truth that can help overcome worrisome thoughts: life is a changing vessel. You are never traveling in the same direction from one day to the next. You might be comfortable now, but your life—and thoughts—is in a constant state of flux. You don't notice it happening, like the faucet that leaks a slow drip.

Over time our lives are moving toward a destination we can't control as well as we would like to. You have two choices here. You can learn to embrace this change. Or, push back against it and create resistance. Worrying about your future won't make it turn out any better. But staying fixed on small actions you can take today has long term benefits.

Distract Your Busy Mind with Focused Thinking

The mind is a sphere of busy activity where your thoughts are concerned. During the day, you will have thousands of thoughts slip into worry and uncertainty:

"What will I do if...?"

"What's the point"

"I'll never be able to do this"

"Everything would be different if only I could..."

As events happen and information is taken in, your thoughts will form logical opinions, ideas, and try to make sense of it all. You make decisions on the fly or sometimes not at all. You might become like a deer frozen in the path of oncoming headlights and can't decide to run, leap or just stand still.

When your thoughts are distracted by worry, fear, uncertainty or confusion, it results in poor performance. You feel the weight of everything pushing down and the pressure to fix it all right now.

In times of mental chaos, how do we cope? You might have tried everything from losing yourself in television to taking long walks to soothe your disturbed mind. You have to practice new tactics and decide what works. You will also discover what doesn't work.

Here are four habits you can put into action when you find yourself losing control of your thoughts. Your goal is to reframe your actions so that you are taking command of the moment.

Read a passage from a good self-help book. I recommend this strategy because it gets you focused onto words that make sense, and not the voices of supposed reason inside your own head. Reading is a great way to get you focused on material that provides a positive spin and can turn random, chaotic thoughts into mindful action.

Write down your goals for now and in the future. Writing in a notebook places the power of creativity into your hands. Try writing down your goals and defining the action steps you are taking this week for each one. Write down the value of achieving your goals. Visualize yourself succeeding already.

Clean out your room. Believe it or not, decluttering your home could be considered a creative course of action. You are removing the things that are taking up space in your home and in your mind. Improving your surroundings can help you keep your thoughts focused.

Implement 30 minutes of focused thinking. Focused thinking is an actionable task you can do at any time, but you need to train your thoughts to know when to act. It is easy to be swept into the tyranny of chaotic thoughts that spiral us down into negativity or helplessness.

Yet, there are times when we are pulled down and through a tunnel of thoughts that feel out of control and there is nothing we can do, no matter what we try.

In such cases, you can ride it out or sit back and observe what is happening. You can still put your meditative practice to work, turn on soothing music, or write out your dreams and aspirations. We don't have to just sit there and take it. You can fight back—even if you think you are losing the fight.

Chapter 3

Reduce Your Worry Habit and Control Mental Fear

"You have powers you never dreamed of. You can do things you never thought you could do. There are no limitations in what you can do except the limitations of your own mind."

— Darwin P. Kingsley

If you observe your own thinking and how your mind interacts with the world, you become a passenger on a wild ride through a theme park. You can be a witness to all the noise and mayhem that comes with a polluted mind that won't stay in the moment.

People are constantly dealing with their thoughts that focus on "getting" and "having" and "becoming." We are attached to owning something or attached to becoming something.

When things are not going as planned, your mind flips into worry mode. Worry is always grounded in the fear of the future. Worrisome thoughts are thoughts we give permission to take control of our state of mind. We worry when we lack trust or faith.

If faith is the belief that things will work out, worry is the belief that everything is in danger of falling apart. It won't work out. You could fail. This could happen or that could happen. Your thoughts start to play out the worst-case scenarios of a bad outcome that results in you ending up empty handed, broke, or alone.

Worry is a broken loop of fear. This is a daily struggle with the mind. You want to trust in something bigger than yourself, but you can't. So, how can you fight back against the loop of fear that worry creates? How do you stop worrying about the future "possibilities" and start living?

You'll need to bring yourself back to the present moment. It starts with reframing your situation and life in a positive framework. Are you seeing the world as a scary, frightful place? Are you afraid of waking up and finding yourself homeless one day? Do you think you'll lose your job next week?

Well, all these things could happen—or none of them could happen. The extent to which they happen is up to you. Most of the worst things that will ever happen to you take place in your mind first... and that's it! Think about the grand symphony of chaos that is constantly conducted inside your mind. But you, as the conductor of your thoughts, can choose how and what to think about. Imagine that. You are the master of your own mind. Remind yourself of this fact and take time to observe your thoughts.

We always have ideas, voices and opinions, mixed with conflicting thoughts based on information we are not entirely sure is correct. How do you separate the good from the bad? How can you trust what is real and what is misleading? How do you stay mindful when your mind wants to wander, explore, and create its own reality without permission?

The strategy I use to filter out the thoughts I don't need is a mental discipline that gets you to focus in on just the present moment. As most of your thoughts jump around and can be in the past one minute and the present the next, this form of mental conditioning—also known as **reframing your thinking portal**—works because it turns down the volume on noisy, intrusive thoughts.

Worry is conditioning your thoughts to fear. If you were raised by fearful parents, and spent most of your youth surrounded by fearful people, then being a worrier will seem the best course of action. This way, you build up your fears of the future and don't take any action for fear of failing.

Right now, make a list of three areas of your life you consistently worry about. Knowing what your triggers are plays a big part in this. Then, when you think about these areas, what thoughts enter your mind? Common themes are thoughts of scarcity, losing something valuable, failing fast, or being embarrassed if your master plan doesn't work out.

You might have fearful thoughts of money or relationships, worry about losing your job or getting ill. These are all legitimate worries. But worry leads to mental paralysis by default, and without taking positive action, you'll end up doing nothing. This ensures the worry habit sticks with its rotation and sets up a loop to capture your thoughts. You must unravel that loop and dismantle the worry habit.

You can empower your thoughts by feeding empowering messages to your mind. It works like the body. If you eat crap and junk food, you're going to feel like a physical garbage can. The mind is no different. Worrisome thoughts generate anxiety. You only get out of it what you feed into it.

Here is how you can eliminate the worry habit right now and gain control over the triggers that set you off.

Worry Thoughts are Fabrications

Worry is believing in false stories that have not come true. You worry about having no money, and yet, there is no evidence to suggest you will always be broke. Maybe you worry about your health and that you might get sick. Well, you will not be healthy forever, you know that. But you have your health today, don't you? Worrisome thoughts are grounded in future fear, like most things we stress about.

Worry is another form of fear. We create most of our fears. They play out in our minds and take over all common sense. What are you worrying about right now? Is it something now or something supposed to happen later?

> *"Freedom is not given to us by anyone; we have to cultivate it ourselves. It is a daily practice... No one can prevent you from being aware of each step you take or each breath in and breath out."*
>
> — **Thich Nhat Hanh,** bestselling author of
> *The Miracle of Mindfulness*

When you feed into the worry habit, you reinforce the false stories that will likely never happen.

From now on, feed your mind the good stuff it really wants. Try these affirmations instead:

- "I am not worried about tomorrow because today is perfect. The here and now is what I have."
- "I always worry about losing my job, but this has never happened to me. I am a good employee and the company I work for values its workers. Why would I think it could happen now?"

Break down your worrisome thoughts and expose these demons for what they are: False fabrications that rarely happen. Worry is a habit, and you can break any habit. But you can make your worrisome beliefs come true, too. If you believe that you will be broke, lose your health, or get divorced, then by carrying this worry around with you can manifest it to come true.

Remember: Thoughts have power and can draw toward you the bad as well as the good. If you think you're going to lose your job, you might show up at work acting like someone who doesn't deserve to be there.

Do you think your spouse is going to divorce you? This worry could cause you to become paranoid. Soon you start to track his or her whereabouts until they catch you planting a GPS unit underneath the car. So, while worrisome thinking is grounded in fantasy, you can manifest your worst nightmares to happen by holding onto these worrisome thoughts.

Negative Thinking: Hardwired for Fear

Positive thinking only works if you truly believe the message you're sending to your brain.

There are a few things I want to say about negative thinking. We tend to see negative thinking as something bad that you should be ashamed of. I'll admit that thinking positively and acting in a positive manner is much better than doing things in a negative way. But, it's a philosophy of mine that negative energy is just as important as positive energy.

How can that be?

You must walk through a mile of slimy mud sometimes before you can get to the green grass on the other end. In other words, being negative and experiencing the suffering that goes with it can be a great motivator for making the decision to change.

Negative thinking—or, "living a negative lifestyle", as I like to call it—is a sign that something is not right with your life. Believe it or not, some people seem to enjoy the attention they receive from negative thinking.

If you have an NMA (i.e., Negative Mental Attitude), and you are not happy with this, deciding to switch over to a positive frame of mind requires that you take intentional action to get your momentum moving.

Some of the world's greatest success stories have come from people who lived through hell and decided to change their lives. You can also look at the people who have everything going for them, and yet, they are unhappy, and it shows in their attitude.

I truly believe that living a positive lifestyle has very little to do with how much you own or how successful you are. It comes down to attitude in every aspect of your life. If all it took was money and popularity, then there wouldn't be any misery with people who seemingly have everything.

Thought and Circumstances: How to Attract What You Want

If you are unhappy with your present circumstances, whether it be your job, relationships, or current state of mind, there is only one way to change it: Think differently. I know this sounds like an obvious piece of advice, but there are reasons for this.

Do you know what happens when you think differently? Things on the outside begin to change. Your situation can only change if you do. Here is why.

Your outer world will always reflect the inner. Your success or failure is based on the success and failure going on inside. Succeed in programming your thoughts for having positive experiences and that is what will happen.

People have been known to alter the course of their lives with a shift in attitude. Can you imagine where you would be if you focused everything you had on thinking with a positive attitude? This isn't to say thinking alone will change you, but without it, we can't follow up with positive actions.

What exactly are positive actions? Some examples are: helping people, working toward goals that get you unstuck, streamlining your efforts to make life worth living for yourself and those around.

The circumstances of this life do not control you. While we can't always choose our circumstances, we can decide how to view them. It is just a matter of fact that bad things happen. Life doesn't go according to plan, and it isn't always fun—no matter who you are or how positive your thoughts may be. But you can train yourself in the best way to deal with it.

Chapter 4

The Impact of Bad Thinking and Creating Peace of Mind

"Choosing to be positive and having a grateful attitude is going to determine how you're going to live your life."

— Joel Osteen

It is not a secret that having negative thoughts can impact your quality of creativity. What really harms creativity is when we dwell on and hold onto our resentments. You see, harboring resentment toward people we don't like—even our enemies—generates a lot of stress.

When you hold onto your hate or create it from concentrating on someone you don't like, this consumes you. The next time you are focusing on disliking someone, check into your feelings. How do you feel? How does your breathing change? Your breathing feels rapid, anxious, and fearful. This is anger. It causes suffering.

Your life is what you make it through the foundation of your thinking. If you feed into thoughts of scarcity and loss, this is what you will experience. Feed into wealth and abundance, and this is going to be your experience. What I discovered years ago is that my life is not a victim of circumstances, as I once believed. It is not built by some random genie in a bottle.

Your life is created by you, and you alone. There are lots of conditions beyond your control, but you don't have to worry about the things beyond your control. Don't spend another moment thinking about the people, events or scenarios that have nothing to do with you. Don't try to change them. Instead, be an observer. Look at how life manifests itself, and the so-called "lucky" people who succeed where others fail.

How often do you point the finger at others and accuse them for your suffering? How many times a day do you wish that others would get their act together and stop making such silly mistakes? I know what this level of thinking does to people. It puts everything in a very small box.

When other people—or circumstances—do not measure up, or fall below our expectations, we start to make judgments and may think negatively about that person with labels and naming. Yes, we have all been at a coffee shop, meeting with friends and taking turns complaining about the day's amount of stupidity that came our way. And while we are doing it, somebody else is complaining about us and our defects.

You are not immune to the gripes of the world, and just as you tear down another person's kingdom, you get blindsided when the same action is taken toward you.

It works both ways. There is only way to stop this.

Put an end to it.

When you feel the need to complain, you must step back and think about who, what, and why. Who are you angry with? Why are you angry with them? What could be done to frame the experience into a more positive mindset? You might be tired of hearing the word "positive" on every page, but, either you are focusing on something with a positive lens or the negative lens (judgments, labels, back alley bad-mouthing).

One path is the easy way: Anyone can complain and gripe, and most do. The other way is less traveled, and few people take it because it requires great effort to retrain yourself, to reframe your way of thinking, and to act in a new way that is altogether different.

Do you enjoy suffering? Do you enjoy watching others suffer? Would you help someone to get over their foolishness if you could? If they did, do you see them being totally different people? I know I do. At least, I do now, but that wasn't always the case.

I spent years hovering over the mistakes and faults of other people, rarely seeing my own. And, when I condemned and labeled them, I could put my own insecurities at rest. But it was a false sense of security. The only real happiness I had is when I stopped expecting others to be something they weren't. The day this realization came to me everything changed.

Everything.

It was as if I had been wearing a pair of glasses that were always blurring my vision, and then, one day, I switched those glasses for better ones. I had reframed, not only my thoughts, but my mindset.

When you expect the world to behave a certain way, and it doesn't, you'll experience stress. That leads to the start of a faulty thought, and from there, a spiral downward begins. Like the links in a chain, one negative thought about something or someone is connected to the next.

By deciding to be present with my mind always, I can bring myself back to a balanced place much quicker than before. I have fewer days to suffer through, and more to enjoy. But it begins here. You can end most of your mental stress and pain here today if you really commit to it.

Too good to be true? The other option is to just let your mind operate on autopilot. Let it do what it does, and you'll get more of the same results. I assume that you don't want to be that person who tears down another's reputation, talks ill of them when they are not around, or wishes them harm because you decided that they deserve it. Be careful what you wish for.

The pendulum swings both ways, and what you dish out comes back to you in larger amounts. Imagine what this would mean if you dished out love, encouragement, or solutions to problems instead of excuses.

Imagine the life you would create for yourself and others if you focused your thoughts on helping people.

What if you gave yourself freely to those people that needed it and expected nothing in return?

Here is another big lesson I learned. I still am learning it, but before I knew about this, I was consumed with my "self", and I focused my thoughts on nothing but me. But you see, "Me" is a lonely figure. "Me" wants the world all to himself. "Me" is an ego that has had its way for far too long. And so, I told "Me" to take a backseat. It had been fed enough in this lifetime.

And so, the journey toward healing began. I learned to empathize and have deeper compassion. I trained my mind to tap into these feelings and think deeply about the obstacles people faced. I could identify with their hardship and seek to discover a solution.

We need to conclude that there are ways we can alleviate suffering— not only our own, but others as well. I am not saying you must stand up and become Gandhi or Dr. Martin Luther King, Jr. or Mother Teresa. Just remember this: Everyone is different and doing their best. They don't act the way we want; they only act *the way they know how*. You can work on tolerance by thinking deeply about other people. Don't worry about what they are thinking about you.

Concentrate on the positive character traits and strengths of everyone you meet. Be ready to help if someone needs it, or offer up sage advice when they are struggling with life's many issues.

Wrong thinking begins as a small drop of water, but soon spreads into a rogue wave. This can lead to depression, social anxiety, and moodiness that transmits from one person to another. Your bad mood isn't just yours if you share it with others. You'll either pass it on or make others flee from you. The one area of my life I needed to adjust was my moods. The vicious cycle of negative self-defeat was my biggest burden.

It would always begin in the morning, while getting the kids ready for school. They wouldn't want to go and would start playing around. I'd have no time but must get them ready. My wife would be yelling, "Why aren't they ready?" My temper would grow short, and it would keep snowballing.

By this stage, I would usually have to walk away and let the kids have their moment. But moods are dangerous. They tend to direct negative energy from within you and project it onto others. It begins with a bad state of mind that focuses on expectations... again.

- *My expectation* is that the kids should always listen and obey.
- **The reality** is they don't.
- *My expectation* is that my co-worker should have asked to use my computer, instead of just helping herself.
- **The reality** is she usually does that to most people; she obviously has no problem with it.
- *My expectation* is traffic should be moving a lot faster than it is today.
- **The reality** is the weather is bad, it's Friday, and there is an accident up ahead.

Expectations are unrealistic. Drop them for a week, a day, or an hour. Focus on just the next 10 minutes if you can! When I learned this, my level of stress was cut in half. When your mind refuses to accept the situation as it is, you are going to experience a great amount of mental stress.

> *"A positive attitude causes a chain reaction of positive thoughts, events and outcomes. It is a catalyst and it sparks extraordinary results."*
>
> **— Wade Boggs**

One of the best observations I have had is in realizing that my thoughts are not necessarily honest all the time. They are deceptive and can manipulate my mind into accepting that everything is true. For instance, when I criticize someone for something they did, or place a label on their behavior or personality, I am convinced that my own judgment is right. I rarely question it.

How could I be wrong if my mind and thoughts have convinced me that I am right, and they are wrong? This is the illusion of reality that escapes most people. We have fallen into the trap of thinking that our own thoughts are the be-all-and-end-all.

The next time you find yourself pointing the finger and criticizing another person, an exercise in empathy is needed. This is the ability to understand and recognize other people from an observer's point of view.

Focus and Wrap Up

By now, you should have a good idea of how to channel your thoughts into effective energy streams that are converted into creative tools. Then, you can channel your thinking toward building a more positive attitude.

Can you imagine how different you could be feeling, acting, and being with the knowledge to channel your thoughts into a creative force? What could you do if you had greater control of your mind? Would you be less scared? Would you do all those things you've always said you would try someday? Go for that new job? Bend your thoughts into a force that you can command instead of being controlled by them.

Your thoughts can be reframed; they just need your direction and guidance. Commit to the mastery of good thinking and you'll never have to worry, feel anxious, or feed into your fearful mind again. After all, every fear is a direct relation to the thought preceding it. Train your mind to stay in the now. Select your thoughts by knowing the circumstances you desire.

Feed your positive thoughts to grow and nurture your soul. Negative thinking has no future. It is a dark tunnel we are always battling against and don't need to enter. You have the tools to set yourself free. You can make decisions based on what your heart desires and not what your mind fears.

The question is: *Are you ready to master your mind and move on to greater things?*

"The more gratefully we fix our minds on the Supreme when good things come to us, the more good things we will receive, and the more rapidly they will come; and the reason simply is that the mental attitude of gratitude draws the mind into closer touch with the source from which the blessings come."

—Wallace D. Wattles

PART II

The Power of a Positive Attitude

Chapter 5

Develop a Positive
Mental Attitude

"It's not the situation, but whether we react negative or respond positive to the situation that is important."

— Zig Ziglar

Do you want to be a totally positive person who attracts success? Makes unbreakable relationships with people from all over the world? Or generates a flow of positive energy that influences thousands to take charge of their lives?

If yes, a positive attitude is your master key to attracting anyone toward you and building the life you always dreamed of owning. It is your positive enthusiasm that opens new doors and creates the opportunity you desire most.

When you are in control of your thoughts, you can master your mindset and turn it into a funnel of positive energy that makes everyday a miracle. Imagine waking up in the morning and all you can feel is this energy to love life and embrace the joy of living. To live this way is not luck or dependent on your circumstances.

It is a choice.

The other choice some people take, unfortunately, is that of harboring a negative mindset. This person is focused on resentment, complaining about life's situations they are stuck with, and spending time thinking about people they don't like.

Developing a negative attitude is like drinking poison. Not only are you hurting yourself, but you are negatively impacting your surroundings and creating misery, anger, and fear. Instead of attracting people to you in a warm embrace, you repel others. The only people you attract are other negative thinkers. Your life becomes a living Hell on Earth and suffering is your fate.

If you neglect to master your thinking and allow yourself to feed the negative monster, suffering will become your lot in life.

A positive enthusiast can have everything in life they desire. But even better—they can give everything to anyone else if they desire it, too. Positive people generate love, warmth, and kindness. People are always happy to see you and want to spend time with you. Your days are a blessing, and time is cherished as you live for the freedom your thoughts create.

Making a choice to develop and project this positive attitude seem like an obvious choice. After all, who wants to choose the path of a negative influencer? Yet, it is easy to fall into the trap of developing a negative mindset. If you are not careful, it can creep up on you without any warning. Therefore, being a positive, outgoing person with a strong, positive mindset always needs to be at the front of your mind.

It takes work, work, and more work to maintain this mindset. Why? Because we live in a world that is filled with powerful negative influencers. To combat this, you must build your arsenal of positive thinking. Your mindset must be determined not to follow the dark path.

Why is it critical to have a positive attitude?

A positive mindset is a real force that delivers. By projecting your mental energy into becoming positive, you are generating your thoughts to take the right actions. What are the right actions? Those are actions that give you a positive result to the questions posed above. Your positive mindset draws the people you need in your life at the most opportune time in a chance to work together toward a worthy objective.

Positive mindset is a creative force packed with natural energy that is pushed out into the world. What you get back from that is a result of your positive thinking. If you want to empower your thoughts, a positive mindset is at the core of this journey.

Your positive mindset draws many advantages:

1. You attract the right people and circumstances to help you succeed;

2. You maintain a peaceful mind that uses mindfulness to stay focused on the present moment;

3. You become financially affluent;

4. Your self-imposed limitations are removed;

5. You experience less stress and more control over your reactions;

6. You live a powerful social life that connects you to amazing people;

7. You see anything as possible, so you are less scared to try new challenges;

8. You gain a positive outlook on the future; and

9. You will laugh more, exercise regularly, eat better, and live longer.

The cost of having a positive attitude is worth millions to your life. I am not just referring to money. It is worth millions of friends, millions of opportunities, and millions of good memories.

If you attitude has been primarily negative, or if there is an area of your life suffering from negative trauma, I can help you with the strategies to get you through it. I know what it's like to have a negative attitude and feel helpless to do anything about it. But you are not helpless.

By accepting failure as the only option, you set yourself up for more failure. You attract the circumstances that bring you the experiences in your life. Will you lead a life filled with joy, love adventure, and wellness? Or, will your life be one filled with anger, constant complaining, and negativity that leads you toward multiple failures without progress.

A negative mindset is at the core of all your failures. If your mindset is stuck in a negative flux, you'll find misery at every turn. Nothing is good enough. There is no point to anything because you can only expect failure from yourself and others. You pass on your negative mindset to those closest to you, robbing them of leading a better life.

Trapped by a negative attitude, you are setting yourself up to suffer. The drawbacks of a negative attitude are:

1. You lack resourcefulness;
2. You have poor mental and physical health;
3. You have high stress levels and are prone to depression;
4. You have "friends" who support your complaints and negative view toward life (i.e., "like attracts like");
5. You maintain a victim persona (i.e., "Why does this always happen to me?");
6. You are subjected to your own ego, driven by self-centeredness;
7. You are plagued by thoughts of excessive worry; and
8. You limit your actions to fit within the confines of a "tiny bubble".

It is in your best interest to draw on the energy of your thoughts by developing the positive attitude of a creative thinker. As we learned in the previous section, your thoughts are not wild animals running loose. You can rope them in and train them.

If your mind is stuck in negativity, that is because you have trained your mind to think that way. You can now reframe your thoughts, too. Your mindset is like Play-Doh. You can mold it into a source of power that serves your mission.

Everything that you have achieved in your life up to now has hinged on your attitude being either positive or negative. Everything that you have depends on your attitude toward the circumstances that govern your surroundings. All the events you experienced, the people you have formed relationships with, and the work you have been doing is a direct result of...

Your mindset.

A positive mental attitude generates positive energy that is creative and contributes to the quality of your lifestyle. It has a profound effect on everyone around you. Having a positive mindset sets you up for all your future wins.

When your mind is focused on the elements of your life that really matter, you will create the positive thoughts and energy that attract every element needed to build a successful life.

You will never be at a loss for friendship or strong alliances when you're focused on helping others. By directing your positive attitude by choice rather than by default, you will be in complete control of the way you view the world. Having a positive mindset creates better success in your work, family, and relationships.

> *"Big thinking precedes great achievement."*
>
> **— Wilferd Peterson**

The choice is yours: You can create your life with a positive mental attitude or a negative one. You can have happiness and succeed, or you can be full of negativity and self-centeredness while failing at most things without trying.

By failing to take responsibility for your present condition, you set yourself up for future pain. If you are focused on fearful thoughts, resentment, and negativity, you will attract these same things into your life. You will naturally become a magnet for the people and events that possess the same negative qualities.

I see people who are in pain, either emotionally or mentally, and most of the time it is because they have poor attitudes and a mindset focused on scarcity. This creates fear, anxiety and the feeling of being helpless and out of control.

But it doesn't have to be this way.

We can change this today.

You are always in total control of your attitude. We don't always create the situations that engage us, but we can decide what to do about it, and how to respond. This makes all the difference when it comes to making serious changes in our lives. When you accept responsibility for your mental state, you are no longer a victim of circumstances. You can create the circumstances—regardless of the attitudes of other people.

After years of creating a negative state for myself, I learned that I could create and change any circumstance by switching my thoughts. Once I figured this out, I became happier, and I discovered a freedom that I never had before. I learned to like myself again, and then I learned to love others. But it wasn't the situation that changed; rather, it was how I was seeing it.

You can change your mindset, too, and then attract better people and situations into your life. Focusing on adding value to your life by being a positive person is only going to create a win-win situation for you. You'll have more friends and opportunities, and a healthier peace of mind. You always have the power to choose. When you give up the right to decide for yourself, choices are forced upon you.

Focusing on positive thoughts and following through with equally powerful actions creates a new attitude shift. Focusing on building a positive mindset is the first thing you must do before anything else. It is the rock-solid foundation for creating a quality lifestyle.

When I stopped blaming everyone else for my problems, took responsibility for my life, and implemented positive thinking into the equation, the good stuff started happening.

Put the development of your mindset at the forefront of your life and you'll be in control of your future in more ways than you can imagine. And, as you will see in the next section, it will clear the way for coming up with great ideas that could potentially change your life.

Chapter 6

The Traits of a Positive Mindset

> *"Positive thinking is a valuable tool that can help you overcome obstacles, deal with pain, and reach new goals."*
>
> **— Amy Morin**

Developing a Positive Mental Attitude (PMA) is crucial to mastering your thoughts. It is the greatest asset you will invest in.

Your decisions, emotions, and the success you achieve depends heavily on your attitude toward the events and people influencing your thoughts. Nothing you work on will deliver the value that a positive mental attitude can give you.

Optimistic About the Future

Optimism is a powerful motivator. Optimistic people are focused on making the future as bright as possible. They are not pulled into events in the past that are over and can never be changed. They move on and scale up.

Optimistic people talk about all the great things they are going to do, and whom they plan to do it with. How about you? What is your level of optimism?

When you take on the attitude of a person with an optimistic outlook, you are saying no to the thoughts that could potentially hold you back; thoughts of worry, anxiety, and self-defeat are no longer entertained.

Optimism generates its own positive force. You don't need any help from the outside when you take on the role of an optimistic adventurer. The world is yours if you aren't afraid to stand up and take it.

Clarity of Life Mission/Believe in the Journey

Clarity in your life is a deeper knowing of what you want, and a willingness to do anything to get it. You are saying to the world, "I am ready to accept anything that you have—good or bad. Bring it on." The road of this journey is not without its challenges. There will be good times and bad times; failures and successes; gains and losses. But if you are clear about *why* you are doing what you are doing, and you stay focused on the path you have chosen; the outcome is not important.

You can only control what you can control, and in most situations in life, that means very little outside of yourself. Stick with your life mission, and if you aren't sure what that is, do what you feel is right in your heart.

Don't wait for someone else to show up and teach you how it's done. Know what to do by clarifying the actions and goals you need to get this thing done.

Building Positive Habits That Reinforce Their Positive Attitude

When it comes to being successful at anything, you'll always find a person's habits are at the core of their success. But not just any habits. You need a system of positive habits that support you and help you build your goals.

For example:

- Waking up early and working out for 30 minutes is a positive habit. It gets you into shape and makes you feel great.

- Writing a book requires you to sit down and write a certain amount of words for a set amount of days until the book is finished.
- Training for a full marathon is about working up to running the pace and being able to complete the marathon, which is about 43 kilometers (i.e., 26.2 miles).

These are habits that you act on every day. When you wake up your mind to act on your thoughts, you can do anything. In addition, it feeds into your positive mindset. You're feeling great about waking up early and training!

Talk Incessantly About Your Goals

When you have a goal that gets you up early in the morning and fires you up right away, you feel great about your life. Did you know that most people walking around have no goals? If you don't have a goal to shoot for, it impacts your attitude. You are more susceptible to moodiness, negative thinking, and are reacting to circumstances instead of creating them.

If you haven't yet taken the time to craft out your life for the next five years, do it right now. If you already know what you want, but you're holding back for fear of failure, the time is now to break this fear and work on what you really want. Nobody is going to show up and just hand you your life. You must reach out and grab it.

"In every day, there are 1,440 minutes. That means we have 1,440 daily opportunities to make a positive impact."

— Les Brown

Once you know what you want, start to talk about it. Tell everyone. Do you want to travel the world and see places you only dreamed of? Talk about it. People may not believe you at first but telling everyone about it sets these goals on fire. It molds your attitude into a funnel of action.

It solidifies your positive attitude by making you more energized and focused on future events. You won't have time to focus on the past and get caught up in old trifles because you'll be too focused on building your future. Your confidence will peak to an all-new level, and you'll give off positive energy everywhere you go.

Take Responsibility for your Life (and Everything Happening in It)

Accepting responsibility for your own life is a massive game changer. Yet, when things go wrong or we are disappointed in someone's behavior, we immediately resort to blame and criticism. Our thoughts revert to old thinking. Remember when you were in school and the teacher asked the class, "Okay, who did it?" when something went wrong? If it were me, I wouldn't raise my hand right away. Who wanted to get punished? But, by not taking responsibility, we leave our thoughts open to suffering.

Complaining is the first sign that you have given up any responsibility for making the situation better. As soon as you start down this path, you come up with all the reasons why you are helpless.

You won't be able to be in a state of positivity if you are focused on building resentment or ill feelings toward other people. This doesn't mean that you must accept another person's behavior as okay. But you *do* have to take charge of your own attitude toward it.

People who take responsibility are in control of destiny. They are empowered by the choices they make. We can't control what is done to us, but we can take charge of our reaction toward it. You can interpret circumstances as events happening to you, but your decisions ultimately determine the outcome.

Building a positive mental mindset has to do with focusing on four specific areas of your life. By creating a healthy balance in each of these areas, you'll experience more peace of mind, harmony, and create more space in your mind for generating creative ideas.

For the rest of this section, we will discuss the areas that you can apply your PMA for the best results.

These are the four pillars of building a positive mental attitude:

1. Your attitude toward past and future events;

2. Your attitude toward yourself;

3. Your attitude toward others; and

4. People, places, and events that challenge your positive attitude.

Chapter 7

Your Attitude Toward Past and Future Events

"It's not the situation that's causing your stress, it's your thoughts, and you can change that right here and now. You can choose to be peaceful right here and now. Peace is a choice, and it has nothing to do with what other people do or think."

— Gerald G. Jampolsky, MD

The past is a time-based perspective. One person can look at their life as a series of tragic events, missed opportunities, or failed outcomes. They are viewing reality through the lens of a negative mindset. People who see the past as a series of negative experiences in which they believe they were made out to be a victim are focused on:

- Relationships that didn't work out;

- Past financial losses;

- A life that just hasn't turned out the way they hoped;

- Missed job opportunities; and/or

- A poor upbringing.

When this happens, it impacts all present moment decisions. This directly influences how your future will turn out.

A person with a positive mindset sees their life as a series of lessons that must be learned through unique experiences that prepare them for the life to come. They know that things like failure are meant to happen, so they can improve the way they do things. Fear is an ally that keeps showing up to challenge them to work harder and not give in.

The best advice I have been given on developing a strong mindset is:

Let go of your thoughts when they come. They will keep knocking on your door and, if you open that door to let them in, you are inviting havoc into your life. Resist the urge to fight back or listen to what your thoughts are saying. Just let them happen. Let yourself happen.

Regardless how you view your personal history, your attitude toward past events plays a powerful role in your success to create a good future for yourself.

First, you must stop struggling. Give yourself a break and be proud that you have made it this far. There is nothing more you can do about past experiences. The mind is always in conflict when it comes to events, either in the past or in the future.

Staying in the moment is the only reality we have. But there is a part of our nature that is addicted to time-traveling—that is, jumping back to revisit old memories or leaping forward to set up predictions for a future that isn't here yet.

The things we have done or not done trigger regret, and the things we have yet to face trigger anxiety and worry. Whether you flip back and forth to past and future realities, neither timeframe is real. They are illusions created by the mind.

Consider these questions:

- Is there anything in your past you deeply regret that is holding you back?

- Is there an experience you had that is hard to let go of?
- Do you see your past failures as learning curves or as permanent failures that define your future reality?
- What would you do over again if you could?
- Taking one of your past failures, how could you turn it into a learning experience that can benefit you today?
- What would you do today if it were your last day on Earth? How would you spend your last remaining hour?

Brooding over failures is the number one reason most people are stuck. Many people are hanging onto old beefs, wishing things had been different, and believing that tomorrow is going to end up just like yesterday. These are the thoughts you need to change if you want to get unstuck. So much of your present attitude is made up of how you still view yesterday's experiences.

Your past doesn't have to be your future.

By moving into the present moment right now, you will realize it is the only timeframe that matters. It's all you have. It's all you will *ever* have. Use this mindset of being present to empower the moment and drive your thoughts into doing what you are focusing on in the now. Develop the attitude that all you have is today, and the past will no longer control you.

When you learn to let go of past mistakes and failed outcomes, you release yourself of that pain. I am not saying that you'll forget about it, but you can learn to accept it and move on.

As William Shakespeare once said, "There is nothing either good or bad, but thinking makes it so."

If your thoughts are trapped in another time zone, your present mindset will remain frozen. When you see every day as a repeat version of what happened 20 years ago, this will become your experience for today and tomorrow. You can change this by refusing to accept past failures as your future.

Eckhart Tolle, the bestselling author of _The Power of Now_, said, "Time isn't precious at all, because it is an illusion. What you perceive as precious is not time but the one point that is out of time: The Now.

That is precious indeed. The more you are focused on time—past and future—the more you miss the Now, the most precious thing there is."

You are the *master-gardener* of your life. It is up to you to take control of your own mind and try to develop the best attitude you possibly can. This will free up your mind to have more creative thoughts and great ideas.

What you think about today is your future tomorrow; your actions today will create your tomorrow, and all the days after. Could it be any simpler? Could you imagine a better way to live? Life isn't a perfect roadmap. Nobody gives us directions to be happy or find joy; it is something we must create for ourselves.

I often catch myself returning to past outcomes and beating myself up by asking, "Why did I do that? I was so stupid. If only I had acted differently, then things would be so different today."

This kind of thinking doesn't create a supportive environment for your positive mindset; it reinforces your disappointment in what you did or didn't do last week, last year, or 10 years ago. And the impact it has on your positive mindset is that you develop a pattern of negative thoughts that just builds over the years, reinforcing your negative mental attitude.

By staying in the present moment, your mind becomes lighter and less cluttered. You can stay focused more easily. You're less anxious. You will develop a deeper peace of mind and feel more grounded by staying focused in your present-moment reality.

Reframe Your Past Experiences

You can reframe your past experiences to view your life in a different way. View everything that happened in your life as a learning curve. Whatever it is that you are holding onto, realize that you did the best with what you had at that time. It couldn't have been any different than what it was. By doing this, you release so much of the stress and tension inside your body.

I am not suggesting you forget about the past. That would be unrealistic. But look at your life as an incredible journey full of all these neat experiences and events that took place (some bad, some good) and reframe everything as, "All that happened was for the best. It didn't work out how I expected it to, but it had a place in my life."

By looking at the experience with a new frame of mind and viewing it differently, you can let go of your old thoughts about failed outcomes. Two people can have the same experience regardless of the outcome and yet, one will view it as a negative event while the other person sees it as a positive one. The experience or event itself is neither positive nor negative and you should try to avoid labeling it as such.

Instead, put it into a constructive frame that supports your beliefs and shifts an otherwise "negative outcome" into a learned experience. Remember that an outcome is only viewed as negative if you were expecting a different result and ended up with something else you didn't want in that moment. Who really knows if the outcome is good or bad?

The scope of this book isn't to teach you everything about reframing, but it is a powerful technique you can implement to shift your attitude (limited beliefs, negative thoughts) about anything so that it builds you up instead of sabotaging you.

Shift your thoughts toward what you are focusing on today. Are there any new relationships you can pursue? Is there something new you can try to increase your skills or knowledge? Is there a goal that has been on the back burner that you want to start working toward? What interesting ideas have you had recently that you would like to put into action?

Your chances of success are exponentially increasing the moment you shift from past events to living in today. This takes diligent practice, but you can do it. There is nothing holding you back.

When you let go of the obsession with controlling the past, it opens a new funnel to create more of what you want in your present life. Stay focused on the present moment because it is the only time in your life that really matters, and it is the only thing you really have any control over. You can manage what is happening right now by making choices in the present situation.

Reframing the Future

The past plays a role in how you live today and in the future. Habits we developed, beliefs, choices, and actions will all affect the future. But the past is over and done with. How can we shift our attitude to work for us in the future? Can we control events that are going to happen?

You do not attract what you *want* in life. You attract what you *are*. We all want something to some extent. Most of the things we desire are just fillers and in most cases are not what we want at all. What you really desire begins with the action you are doing in the moment. There are no magic tricks or strategies for creating a nice future for yourself and your family. It begins here with doing what you love to do.

For example:

- You want to be a writer? You make it a habit to write. You could be doing that now.
- You want to spend more time with your children? Plan to go to the beach or park. Do it today or plan for it first thing tomorrow.
- You want to change careers because your job is not in line with the work you really want? Think deeply about the work you really enjoy and start to work on it. Brainstorm your ideas for the work you want and figure out how you can make a living from this.

Just as the past can be reframed in a positive way, the future that holds everything you ever want is ready the moment you get to work today.

To reframe your future in a mindset that reinforces a good outcome, consider these causes of mental stress.

Predicting a Bad Outcome

Have you ever heard someone say something like, "This never works out for me"? Such people are basing their success tomorrow on what happened last week. What they are saying is, "Okay, so I failed twice at this already; what is the point in trying again?"

Using Past Evidence to Make False Predictions About Tomorrow

This kind of thinking sets us up for failure in the future, as well. Your future is what happens when you make present choices. If you want to do something tomorrow, you must start doing it today. When it comes to mindfulness thinking, we can make conscious choices on which thoughts we will obey, ignore, or create.

Failure to Focus

Tame your thinking to focus on the actions you want to do. By doing this we can eliminate procrastination, stop doing the things we don't like, and remove a great deal of mental anguish accumulated through overwhelming ourselves. You can always step in at any time and say, "Wait, I don't like this train of thinking. Let's stop doing it this way and do it like this instead."

Negative Self-Talk

You can fix the voice inside that speaks to your mind. It is the voice that can remove you from the clutter of the future. The pattern is created by the worry caused by unknowing; the stress caused by not knowing how to deal with it; and the overwhelming feeling created by not knowing how you can deal with so much.

Staying present means letting go of all that negative thinking. Your thoughts can't focus on the future and be present at the same time. I recommend practicing how to let things go as they happen.

Here is a simple three-step process I use that works:

1. **Bring your consciousness into the present moment right now.** As soon as you are aware that you are in the present moment, your thoughts are present as well. Your mind will follow your lead.

2. **Ask yourself: "What am I doing right now? What am I working on?"** We are fearful that we will not have everything we want in the future. We fear loss and scarcity. People are terrified of not having enough money to retire, or that they will lose their job someday. You can work on your life plan right now that will place you in a better position to deal with these things when they happen. How can you better manage your finances today, so you are not thinking about it and creating fearful thoughts?

3. **Ask yourself: "Who is the most important person in my life right now? What can I do now to reach out to them or spend more time together?"** It is stressful to realize that people we love will grow up, get older, and eventually disappear. This is unavoidable. But we can think about how best to serve them right now. This gives you memories you can cherish someday when you want to look back and remind yourself of a time you enjoyed the company of friends, family, and your children.

Taking this conscious action now is the best method for removing your fears, stress, and overwhelm about future events. I am not suggesting you shouldn't think about your future but, rather, set yourself up for the best possible future with present mindful actions.

Key Takeaways

- Stay focused on today's tasks and objectives; enjoy the precious moments that today brings.
- Focusing on the past means you'll be less likely to see the present opportunities.
- Work on the tasks at hand and not the ones completed; reframe old beliefs and ideas by looking at them differently. It is not what happened, but how you perceive the outcome.
- Learn to forgive yourself for past mistakes and failures. Nobody has had a perfect life, and your so-called failures are part of the learning curve cycle. Be proud of what you have done with your life up to now.
- Think about the course of your life for the next 30 minutes. Ask yourself, "Where do I want to be in one year? Five years? 10 years from now?"

Chapter 8

Your Attitude Toward
Other People

> *"Choose the positive. You have a choice. You are the master of your attitude. Choose the positive, the constructive."*
>
> **— Bruce Lee**

Your attitude toward yourself is the second area that contributes to the quality of your positive mindset.

It amazes me how people treat themselves as if they were their own worst enemy. We might drink too much, smoke, or commit other acts that sabotage our characters, health, and put ourselves at risk regardless of the potential consequences.

Your attitude toward yourself plays a vital role in the quality of your lifestyle you create. By working on developing a positive attitude for yourself, you'll overcome all levels of low self-esteem and boost your confidence.

Your mindset toward yourself is the foundation for all your success. It is simple, really. Maintain a positive mindset and you create a quality lifestyle that is rich beyond anything you ever dreamed of (no fluff—it's true).

If you are stuck in a negative state and express this attitude toward the people and situations in your life, you can only blame yourself when things go wrong. This isn't to say that only good stuff happens when you maintain a positive attitude. The bad stuff will happen too. What makes the difference is how you perceive the experience, and how you choose to deal with it. There is nothing right or wrong, but your thinking makes it so.

Create a Positive Mindset Toward Yourself

The attitude you have toward yourself defines the actions you take daily. When I was angry and negative, I had a poor self-image. This led to taking action that defeated my life.

When I worked toward shifting my attitude, surprisingly enough, the good stuff that I always dreamed about started happening. I don't believe it was a coincidence. Therefore, your attitude—not just toward others but also toward yourself—is a paramount factor in determining your overall joy and satisfaction.

Love Yourself Unconditionally

Above all else, you should love yourself unconditionally. When your attitude toward yourself is healthy, and you communicate to yourself in a positive way, you naturally treat others well and your attitude toward them is warm and accepting. People pick up on this. If you have a poor attitude, this emanates from within and negative people will be attracted to you. The winners are not going to waste one minute in your company.

In his book called *Love Yourself Like Your Life Depends On It*, author Kamal Ravikant says, "As you love yourself, life loves you back. I don't think it has a choice either. I can't explain how it works but I know it to be true."

Many people only like themselves when they accomplish something or have done something worthy of love. It comes from social conditioning. When you are good, you are rewarded; but if you're bad or you fail a test in school, you are deemed to be deserving of punishment somehow. We are not taught to love ourselves unconditionally but to respond to a reward system that focuses on conditional love.

When it comes to creating a positive image for yourself, focus on liking yourself...a lot. Then, focus on loving yourself. It doesn't matter what you accomplish, how much you own, or who is impressed with you. What matters is that you can look at yourself each day and say, "I'm glad I'm me." Seems silly?

Try it for a week. Try it for a month. Try it for the rest of your life.

Observe the Negative Labels You Place on Yourself

Take notice of the times you are labeling yourself harshly. This is where positive affirmations can play a key role in shaping your mindset to speak to yourself in a gentler, more positive way.

If you are in the habit of feeding negative messages to yourself (e.g., "What an idiot I am!"; "I'll never succeed!"; "I'm always failing!"), you have to swap the little voice that threatens, hurts, and puts down for a voice that is supportive and fills you with encouragement.

You create labels when you have disappointed yourself or think you failed somehow. And maybe you did. But who doesn't fail? Who doesn't make mistakes? Who isn't human? Who has a perfect life? You can give yourself a break. Make a list of positive affirmations and practice saying them several times a day.

Shift this attitude and you shift your thoughts too. You can start with very simple steps. Step up to the plate and put a stop to the committee in your head. Silence it once and for all. Recognize it for what it is: the ramblings of mad voices operating without your consent.

This is the ego of the mind, and its mission is to control your will by filling your head with false beliefs. You can put a stop to it by recognizing when it's happening and then saying, "Okay, enough. Get lost."

Seriously, you have the power to turn it off. The voices are yours to command, not the other way around.

Establish Your Mindset at the Beginning of Each Day

What really worked for me and countless others I know is waking up with the right attitude. In other words, wake up on the "right side" of the bed. So many times, I either went to bed with the wrong frame of mind or woke up with it.

If you start the day on a bad note, it is going to stay with you throughout the rest of the day, unless you get a handle on it first thing in the morning.

It is crucial to set up your positive mindset for success early in the morning. I can't tell you how many times I have woken up angry, bitter, or dreading the day that I was about to have. It starts with a negative thought and that one thought trickles into more until I have an avalanche of negativity even before I get to breakfast.

So, how can you wake up with a good attitude that lasts throughout the day?

I do four things:

1. **Exercise for the first 20 minutes.** I do two sets of leg squats and two sets of push-ups; 20 reps. You can do whatever exercise you want to: yoga, tai chi, shadow boxing, or a simple series of stretches. The key is to exercise for 20 minutes.
2. **Free flow writing for 20 minutes.** Write down whatever comes to your mind. These are called "morning pages"—an idea I adopted from *The Artist's Way* by Julia Cameron. This is an amazing exercise to clear your mind. It also flushes out any ideas you might have.
3. **Read for 20 minutes.** Choose a good self-help or read your list of affirmations and positive quotes. At the back of this book, I've listed my favorite books. By reading for 20 minutes a day, you could get through two books a month.
4. Lastly, **drink a glass of water and eat a good breakfast.**

I can't stress enough how this simple system at the beginning of each day saves me from having a miserable day. When I wake up full of worry, anger, resentment, or focusing on a negative experience I had, the day is wasted.

It is very difficult to bring yourself back to a positive state of mind if you start the day off badly. Start it off right, and no matter what happens that day, you'll be able to handle it much better.

Key Takeaways

- Make consistent effort to break any bad habits that are damaging to your mental health and body.
- Make a list of your good qualities and remind yourself what they are.
- Avoid things such as personal labels, self-pity, or envy.
- Remember that you can only be defeated by yourself, and your attitude toward yourself is paramount above all else.
- Be aware of those bad days you have; let yourself have a bad day, but before you go to bed, feed your thoughts with positive affirmations and some good motivational material.
- Create a worthy goal for yourself and spend some time each day working toward this goal. Learn to recognize and filter out anything that gets in your way of maintaining a positive attitude such as negative thoughts and self-criticism.
- Stay away from reading "junk news" and articles that don't contribute to your positive mindset.
- Remember: It isn't the size of the obstacle that defeats you. It's your attitude toward the obstacle that matters.

Chapter 9

People, Places, and Events That Challenge Your Positive Attitude

"In times of great stress or adversity, it's always best to keep busy, to plow your anger and your energy into something positive."

— Lee Iacocca,
former American Automobile Executive

Even the most positive and inspiring people are challenged by the trials and tribulations of everyday living. Maintaining a positive attitude and outlook can be challenging when the rest of the world seems hell-bent on making your life difficult. But that is the reality: Life isn't always easy. When you face it with an optimistic mindset, people and situations are easier to deal with.

There are many situations that will challenge your positive mental attitude. Maintaining a positive mental attitude can be tough when you are surrounded by adversity. Adversity could be something simple—like another driver cutting you off in traffic—or more complex relationship issues. Maybe coworkers want you to solve their problems for them, or someone has an emergency that has nothing to do with you, but you are the one expected to take care of it.

There is a whole list of things that can happen every day that are going to take your positive attitude and put it to the test. The question you need to ask yourself in these situations is, "What am I going to do?"

What did Gandhi do when he was faced with adversity?

Gandhi lived a simple life. He never had much, and he never needed much. He wore simple robes and only ate as much as he needed to. He lived in a state that many deemed as poverty, but this is *how he chose to live.*

His mission and purpose were to free his nation from the British rule. How did he stay positive and strong when faced with threats, and the possibility of being killed? How could he maintain such a level of spiritual and mental freedom when his life his people were at stake? How could *anyone?*

You don't have to be Gandhi to deal with life's difficulties, but you can try putting yourself in someone's shoes by visually imaging what they would do. How would (insert the name of a person you admire) handle this? What would they do?

When I have a bad day or I come up against someone who is giving me grief, and I would like to do nothing more than get into it and handle the situation with an aggressive attitude, I stop and ask myself this one question: "What would Gandhi do?" It might sound like a crazy question to ask yourself, but seriously, it calms me right down.

Why? It changes my whole perspective. Instead of not knowing the best solution and wondering, "What am I going to do?" I ask a question that shifts my frame of mind toward somebody I know that could handle this problem.

You can replace Gandhi with anyone you like: Mother Teresa, Jesus Christ, Buddha, or the Dalai Lama. It can be someone you know in your family or neighborhood that you respect because they are a positive influence on your life.

Whomever it is, use that person as your "perfect model" to deal with a difficult situation, person, or a challenging problem. When I ask that question, the answer eventually comes, and I'm less likely to lose my temper, overreact, or lash out in anger.

Try this strategy in any situation that you find challenging. With practice, you will be able to manage your emotions much better and maintain that positive outlook that you have worked so hard to create.

What are the difficult situations you are facing now?

Not a day goes by when you are not going to be faced with some problem, crisis, or situation that takes you out of your happy spot:

- You are driving and feeling the power of a happy moment when your car dies.
- You get a bill for $3,000 you must pay by the end of the month, but you only have fifty dollars in the bank.
- A friend is getting divorced, and you start to worry about your own marriage.
- Delayed trains, planes, and automobiles: In a land full of chaos, staying in your happy spot is challenging.

Pick one of these situations and map out your solutions list. Make a list of what you can do to handle it. You can't always prepare yourself for everything that could happen but take time to visualize problems that might occur. Then, try to work out a solution to each problem.

By running through "situation simulations," you can train your mind to be better prepared for handling tough problems when they come up. You'll have less stress and be more confident to take on whatever life throws at you.

"Cutting it Loose" Strategy

There are just some things that we can't do anything about. Yet, we might hold onto them because we feel obligated or responsible. I say, if it has nothing to do with anything you did directly, cut it loose from your life.

Why deal with other people's problems if they aren't your issues to begin with? I often get so caught up in things happening around me when I try to do too much. You don't have to solve the world's problems. Start with your own and then help someone else whenever you can.

When faced with a situation that I can't deal with, I use a thought technique called "cutting loose".

With your mental scissors, imagine cutting this thing loose and watching it fall away into darkness (I imagine it falling away into nothingness). Try this as many times as it takes. Letting old outcomes go is one way to free up your mind. And the more free space you open in your mind, the lighter you'll feel.

Remember: Your mind is full of the accumulation of so much stuff over the years and it needs to be dumped out every now and then. When you hold onto old ideas, thoughts, and gripes, it turns to anger and causes stress. You will get headaches more frequently and start losing sleep.

I spend 15 minutes meditating every night before going to bed. For years, I didn't meditate—even though I had heard so much about the benefits, and how great it is for you. When I started, it was hard to keep it going as a habit, but gradually, it worked. It puts my mind at ease, and I don't go to bed holding all that mental junk inside. Dump the junk out of your head if it's taking up valuable space.

Control Your Reactions

Your reaction to any person, place, or thing is under your control. Nobody can make you act in any manner. When you say, "He made me angry," what you are really saying is, "He did something I didn't approve of, and I made the decision to react this way."

The only way that you are really going to develop a firm, solid attitude is through practice, so use these challenges to exercise. There is no better way to develop this discipline than going out into the world and saying, "Okay, give it to me. What have you got?"

Over the years, I have developed a considerable tolerance toward a lot of people and situations that years ago would have had me spinning. I still get into gripe mode and wish that these people or problems did not exist, but, then again, where would I be if they didn't.

The world is not going to bend for you or me. You must be the rock in the river that can build up enough personal power to stand strong against the current and let it run around you. A great strategy I use every day is to step out of the mayhem and become an observer of everything I see happening around me.

> *"There is little difference in people, but that little difference makes a big difference. The little difference is attitude. The big difference is whether it is positive or negative."*
>
> **– W. Clement Stone**

For example, certain times of the day, I'll break away from my desk and the monotonous habit of just staring at a computer screen and start to listen to everything going on around me. You can see people so immersed in their little world, running around putting out fires, looking busy when they are not, or looking for something to engage their attention. I use this observance technique to bring myself into the reality of the world around me.

You can do it anywhere. Next time you go outside, stand off to the side on a busy street and watch everybody as they run here and there, using smartphones, communicating, arguing, immersed in their little world as it is going on around them. We are all a part of this.

What I discovered from this technique is that the world is not about me. When you are in the thick of a busy day, doesn't it feel like everything going on around you is somehow about you? When I stopped taking things so personally, it made it easier to accept and deal with.

Most of what happens to us, and how we deal with it, is perception. Two people can go through the exact same experience, and yet come out of it completely different. One person is stressed out, anxious, and needs medication to calm down. The other person shrugs it off and says, "Oh, well, that was fun." Most of what happens in our day-to-day lives has nothing to do with us in many cases, but people get too involved, and they invite these problems in.

Key Takeaways

- Create a script in your head that directly communicates with the person who is causing you grief. This is very powerful. This is very important and can sustain your positive attitude for long periods of time.
- Use the "What Would Gandhi Do" technique. Ask yourself, "What would (name here) do in this situation?" This is a powerful strategy for getting clarity when things are really difficult.
- Use the "cutting it loose" strategy for dealing with people or situations that you are not responsible for. When you just can't think about the problem in your life at the moment, you have to cut it loose.
- Remember that you cannot change the attitude or control the behavior of other people. They are going to do what they do. You can only control your reaction to it.
- Take some time out and apply the "observance technique." Watch everything happening around you. Then, when you step back into it, you have a wider perspective of the world and the people as they act and react.
- Quit taking things personally.

Chapter 10

Strategies to Build Your Positive Attitude

> *"You've done it before and you can do it now. See the positive possibilities. Redirect the substantial energy of your frustration and turn it into positive, effective, unstoppable determination."*
>
> **— Ralph Marston**

In this chapter, here are some action tasks you can implement to live a more positive lifestyle and start working on increasing your positive attitude. Don't worry about the days when you have "downtime", and your negative thinking starts lurking around. When you do the things that make you feel good, you'll naturally pick yourself up.

By doing at least three of these tasks every day, you'll develop a powerful mindset and empower your thoughts to become creative devices.

Here is a list of strategies you can try in developing your positive mental attitude.

Use Positive Affirmations

Read positive quotes and affirmations. Keep these quotes handy so that you can refer to them every day. I choose five quotes every night and read them several times throughout the day.

Wake Up Early

Your brain is most active in the morning. Try getting up earlier than usual, reading for 20 minutes, or exercising. You can write a blog post or take your dog for an early walk. The time spent in the morning can be your most important time of the day because it sets the tone for your PMA throughout the rest of the day.

Meditate Twice a Day for 15 Minutes Each Session

Meditation clears your mind and enhances your concentration. By meditating, you gain greater control over your mental functions, and an increased ability to focus. It reduces your stress, improves your health, and reduces negative energy, while increasing your capacity to think up great ideas. Schedule in 15-minutes a day for meditation practice.

Learn Something New

A mind that is stagnant stays stuck in old beliefs and habits. Learning new skills and staying open to better ways of doing things frees your mind space up and makes room for more advanced learning. You could learn new skills to increase business opportunities or improve the quality of your relationships with friends and family.

By increasing your skills through committing to constant and never-ending improvement, you attract the people and situations that add greater value to life.

Write Down Three Positive Points About Someone You Struggle to Get Along With

If Gandhi could take on the British Empire and practice forgiveness when surrounded by adversity, you can try to forgive one person and their defects. Write down the person's name. Then, write down three things they do well and praise them for it.

If you can't approach someone in person, you can write everything down and read it out loud. Visualize the person is there in the room with you. You will experience an amazing feeling of "letting go" with this activity.

Read Books on Personal Development and Mindset Growth

Try to schedule reading time every day and do it for at least 20 minutes. I spend upwards to an hour most days reading something. This has been a major contributor toward developing my positive attitude. Reading isn't just something you should do when you have time; it should be a part of your daily routine.

You can pencil in the time to read, instead of just doing it when you have time. This one daily habit of reading will set a positive tone for your mindset.

Here is a short list of amazing books I recommend:

- *The Miracle Morning* by Hal Elrod
- *Awaken the Giant Within* by Anthony Robbins
- *Maximum Achievement* by Brian Tracy
- *Think and Grow Rich* by Napoleon Hill
- *The Magic of Thinking Big* by David J. Schwartz
- *The Power of Positive Thinking* by Norman Vincent Peale
- *The 7 Habits of Highly Effective People* by Stephen R. Covey
- *The Success Principles: How to Get from Where You Are to Where You Want to Be* by Jack Canfield
- *Creative Visualization* by Shakti Gawain
- *Essentialism: The Disciplined Pursuit of Less* by Greg McKeown

Now, add at least 10 more books you would like to put on your reading list!

> *"If we're growing, we're always going to be out of our comfort zone."*
>
> **– John C Maxwell,**
> bestselling author of *Fail Forward*

Write Out Your Goals

Schedule one hour a day for the next week to write down your goals for the next five years. Which goal will have the biggest impact on your life this year? Which goals do you have for this month? You can create goals for every area of your life: health, wealth, relationships, and travel. Put aside at least three hours to totally map out your goals for the next 20 years.

Focus on Empowering Your Thoughts

Try to keep your thoughts positive, constructive, and clear of clutter. Watch out for negative thoughts and put a stop to them when they happen. Avoid labeling or buying into negative discussions that focus on complaining, bickering, and petty issues that harm others. Observe the thoughts you have about people and situations.

Turn Off the TV

We spend far too much time watching television. I won't suggest stopping it altogether because it is good to relax and watch a movie from time to time. But any more than 30 minutes a day, and you are killing time that you can never get back.

Instead of watching endless hours without any self-control, schedule your TV time after your other stuff is finished. For example, Saturday night is my DVD-movie time. I watch a movie every Saturday evening. When I watch TV as a default habit just to kill time, it becomes the only thing I do. During the rest of the week, I unplug it and don't turn it on at all.

"There is a thinking stuff from which all things are made, and which, in its original state, permeates, penetrates, and fills the interspaces of the universe."

—Wallace D. Wattles

Are You Enjoying
Empower Your Thoughts?

Try listening to the audiobook as narrated by Joe Hempel
Click on the image to <u>BUY NOW</u>.

<u>Empower Your Thoughts: The Audiobook</u>

PART III

Transform Your Thoughts

Chapter 11

Internal Communication and The Language of Thought

> *"Much talking is the cause of danger. Silence is the means of avoiding misfortune. The talkative parrot is shut up in a cage. Other birds, without speech, fly freely about."*
>
> **— Saskya Pandita**

The language you are using has a direct influence on both your thoughts and their corresponding mindset. But this isn't only through spoken word. Communicating with yourself internally is a key component of creating clear, positive thoughts.

The Power of Internal Voices

Your internal voice has a tone and vocabulary of its own. In most cases, what we think and what we say are very different. But the result is the same. If you think words of anger and resentment through your "internal critic", your thoughts and emotions are affected.

What you think is how you feel—regardless if you express your emotion externally. We can be in a foul mood inside but still hide it on the outside. But we are now suffering with those negative emotions internally.

Your internal communication is a powerful influence. By selecting the language you use with yourself and others, you are choosing to become the master of your own thinking. The words you choose to use and the tone of the language you address others, directly impacts how you think and feel.

People who are generally angry, moody, or stuck in a negative state are communicating with their thoughts in the same way. It is natural. We think first and speak later.

How to Communicate with Your Mind

As you saw earlier, it sometimes feels like your mind is taken over by an alien force, and you lose all control over what you think—and even say. But you know this is just an illusion of the mind. It is another trick to keep you confused.

You can abruptly put an end to this confusion by training your mind to communicate. Instead of letting it run away with your thoughts and fill your mind with fear and scarcity, recognize that the voices speaking to you belong to your subconscious.

Earlier in the book we talked about mindfulness and the importance it can play in your life. Well, spending small chunks of time trying to calm your thoughts is an investment in your mental health. When it comes to the language you pass between your thoughts and mind, you can monitor your internal dialogue, and gain better control over it.

Are you thinking angry thoughts? Are your words shrouded in frustration or have negative connotations? Are you filling your head with fearful thinking?

Your "internal voice" is a deceptive animal. It can appear out of nowhere and twist thought into your own worst enemy. Imagine this: **Your biggest enemy isn't out there, looking for a way to get to you. You have this enemy in your mind.** As soon as you see this for what it is, you are building that bridge to your freedom.

People spend years trying to build happiness into their lives. They find ways to earn more money, start new relationships, change jobs, or take sporadic shopping sprees. They feel good for a while and then they find themselves back to where they started. Why?

The solution is never "out there." The moment you come to see your internal enemy hiding behind the folds of your thoughts, it is like a beacon is turned on in your mind. You start to think more clearly. You are calm and restful. Anxiety and fear melt away.

By reading this book, you have been given all the tools and tactics needed to confront this self-defeating enemy of the mind. The question is, will you win or lose? Do you want to be happy or miserable? Will you give in or give up?

If you want the enemy in your head to control your thoughts and internal voice, while crushing your mind in the process, then here is what you continue to do:

- Watch TV for hours a day, ignoring your thoughts and filling your mind with senseless entertainment;
- Read the news and feel depressed about all the bad drama out there;
- Complain constantly about the people whom you don't like;
- Use words like "I hate," "I can't stand," or "I wish she would only…";
- Blame someone else, or your circumstances, for your failures and lack of success;
- Release your anger by yelling at people when you don't get your way; and/or
- Believe that "This is just the way it is," and continue to do what you have always done.

Our actions up to this point have been defeating us. If you want to succeed, then start with recognizing the enemy in your mind. Visualize this beast and how it just appears in your thoughts. Of course, we have heard the saying, "The greatest trick the devil ever pulled was convincing the world he didn't exist." Well, our mind has a devil, a monster, a monkey, or whatever you wish to identify it as. The moment you recognize its existence, you can turn everything around.

So, the question is: "How do I do this?"

You already started when you decided to read this book.

Here are two strategies to help you communicate with your thoughts and heal your mind from falling into a state of distraction. You can continue your journey toward mastering your thoughts right now.

Do What you Love and Schedule This Activity into Your Day

We all have something we love doing—or used to love doing—but it is rarely a priority with everything else going on. When I started writing again after 20 years of just thinking about it, I had to make time for it.

There was always something else I could have been doing, and when I was bored, I just switched on the TV. But by scheduling 30 minutes a day, I could get a book written in two months. Now, what could you schedule into your day for 30 minutes?

Here are a few examples:

- Exercise for 30 minutes
- Draw or paint
- Practice a musical instrument
- Write your thoughts in a journal
- Cook your favorite food

Do what you love, and you will cure negative thinking or time-wasting distractions. They naturally fall away.

> *"Choose a job you love, and you will never have to work a day in your life."*
>
> **— Confucius**

Set a timer and get everything ready before you start. Then, work on your one thing for 30 minutes. You can take a break, and, if you have more time, continue to work on this for another 30 minutes. Doing what you love creates a healthy space for your thoughts to flow. Put yourself in a happy state, and your thoughts will follow.

Our actions have direct influence on how we feel, and our emotions can drive the quality of thought to a higher level. During this time your thoughts are not distracted. You can think clearly and enjoy a state of focused work.

Quiet Time Focused on Your Thoughts and Feelings

We all try to wind down after a day at work or a day full of family activity. Before crawling into bed, exhausted, or checking your email, set up 15 minutes of quiet reflection. During this time, you will think about your gratitude for aspects of your life.

Ask yourself questions that get you thinking about your purpose: "Why am I here? What am I working toward? Who am I right now? What negativity am I experiencing at this moment? Who do I love? Who do I resent?"

Get into the habit of talking with your mind. Why listen to all the senseless noise and chatter? The more you listen to this, the more it drives you crazy. You need to turn this down or turn it off. Practice saying a mantra or use positive words that reinforce your love for yourself and the environment you are in.

You can play meditative music while you do this or just sit in silence. This is different from a form of meditation, wherein you are focusing on your thoughts to better understand your present state. During the day, with so much going on, it is a real struggle to find this state of quietness.

To start, we must set it up, so we can put ourselves in a quiet state of thought-awareness. As you practice this more, you will soon be able to do it even if you are in a boardroom or a classroom. Ideally, connecting with your thoughts by recognizing how they are communicating with you is a powerful exercise.

Leaders need to be able to do this so they can avoid overreacting under pressure. Athletes must do this so they can remain calm when under pressure to perform. Parents should be able to do this so they can communicate with the family during difficult times.

Build this quiet place within yourself and you can go there at any time. Associate this with a certain piece of music or perhaps a quote or positive affirmation that gets you there.

Build a bridge to this place, and when you feel anxious, stressed, or fearful, you can go there to get balanced again.

Chapter 12

The Positive Impact of Words and Affirmations

> *"Small shifts in your thinking, and small changes in your energy, can lead to massive alterations of your end result."*
>
> **— Kevin Michel**

As we learned in the previous chapter, self-talk is about getting your mind right and filling your thoughts with positive messages. To become a person of influence and to encourage, inspire, and lead others, you must be right with yourself. You must be able to communicate your thoughts in a positive way to your own mind before you can communicate your thoughts and ideas with the world.

Your words are powerful vehicles of expression. They can build a person up or tear them down all in the same minute. A choice set of words vented in anger can have a lasting impact that is remembered for years to come.

A positive act of encouragement has the same effect by sticking in the mind of the person on the receiving end. Think of a time when someone said something encouraging to you about an achievement. How did you feel at the time? Without a doubt you were elevated and confident to try harder.

Visualize that moment and you can probably still connect with the other person's thoughts. You see, not only do you impact your own thoughts, but you can influence the thinking of others. In a world rife with negative messages in our society and media, the one thing that stands out is your ability to positively influence other people.

This is the hallmark of a real leader who cares. You can do this with your family, co-workers, or the people you meet every day, who serve you coffee, wait on you at a restaurant, or take your call on the phone.

Positively Impact Others with Power Words and Phrases

Have you ever listened to motivational speakers as they speak to the audience? Try listening to the recordings of Tony Robbins, Jim Rohn, or Zig Ziglar. You can feel the positive force behind the voice. They speak to the people as someone who loves their crowd. You know they genuinely care about the people who are out there listening to every word they say.

Therefore, they have millions of followers. People want to hear what they have to say. You might think it is all just "woo-woo" or "rah-rah," but what would be the alternative? Someone telling you that the world is a scary place, and you'd better look out for Number One?

This is a message many people buy into, and in believing it, they act on it. When we are exposed to the negative messages that are reinforced by action, this becomes part of our identity. People say things like, "oh yeah, she just looks out for herself," or "He's so critical of others."

The identity people associate with began as a thought that transformed into action. Your actions are direct orders from your thinking. But you can change your identity by changing the way you speak to people. Switch the negative language over to words that motivate, inspire, and excite them. Soon, people are saying things about you that sound like this:

- "She is so full of positive energy. I feel good just being around her."
- "Something he said really resonated with me. What an impact!"
- "What she said really changed my perspective and my life. I wish I'd had more of this growing up."

For years, I was not a positive-approach person. It was a real struggle to speak well of people—even when they truly deserved it. By recognizing this trait as something I didn't want, I switched my mindset to start acting like a positive influencer.

This started with the words I spoke to people and how I used them. I traded hate for love and criticism for optimism. I would catch myself when I started to tear someone down in conversation and immediately keep the opinion to myself, or, find at least one good thing to say about them, if nothing else.

It takes time, but gradually, you can choose to communicate this positive thought energy.

Here are six strategies we can put into practice right away. This will help you to develop a larger vocabulary focused on motivational words and phrases that can change lives.

1. **Refrain from speaking negatively about anyone.** This includes complaining about someone's behavior or criticizing for mistakes made.
2. **Focus on power words.** Use words that are filled with encouragement. "I can," "You can do it," or use the quotes found in this book if it is hard for you to come up with anything.
3. **Focus on future plans and goals.** Get excited about a project or a goal someone is trying to achieve. Get into it and ask if they need any help to achieve that goal. Encourage your listeners to work hard and keep pushing forward no matter the obstacles ahead.
4. **Frame the moment in a positive light.** Now is the best time to try anything. Don't wait for the day to be perfect before you start to live, and don't let procrastination destroy your opportunity to be great.
5. **Eliminate the list of negative words and phrases from your speech.** Words such as "impossible," "It can't be done," "It's a stupid idea," "I hate...," or "I'll never have that." Most limits are self-imposed. In fact, almost *all* of them are. We fail ourselves first before the world has a chance to do so. If someone is using these

words as excuses for not taking direct action when it's needed, call that person out on it.

6. **Avoid talk focused on trivial events you can't control.** There are so many events and happenings daily that influence our emotional state... *if we let them.* Many of these things can be filtered out. We get focused on the acts of others, and how they directly impact our lives—even if we've never met them or had anything to do with the event itself.

Remember the serenity prayer, one of the most powerful expressions you'll ever learn:

> *"God, grant me the serenity to accept the things I cannot change, the courage to change the things I can, and the wisdom to know the difference."*

You don't have to be in recovery to recite this several times a day. It works when we are caught up in trivial garbage. In the end, how important is it to get caught up in a negative spin cycle of chaos?

In most cases, it isn't important at all...unless you make it so.
Your words are a direct reflection of what is inside your mind. You can't be a positive thinker and talk negatively about your life. Action follows thought.

Get your thoughts in order, and the positive mindset will follow. Get your thoughts in order, and you'll always be acting, speaking, and living in the right way.

Chapter 13

Harnessing Thought and Mastering Emotion

"Find a place inside where there's joy, and the joy will burn out the pain."

— Joseph Campbell

One of the most direct ways to master your emotions is to have control over your thoughts. Every emotion is accompanied by a thought at first. You must understand that to control your emotions, you must think about the feelings you *want* to experience.

This gives you a major advantage over most people. Most people don't take time to consider these concepts. Remember that all your thoughts are working to create something: **emotion**. Your emotions rise from the thoughts you have.

We can test this very easily. Right now, think of a situation or a person that makes you angry. This could be a resentment you are still holding onto—maybe someone just broke up with you and you're still mad— or a manager who is extremely difficult to work for in your current job. Think about that person in all their entirety. Now, how do you feel?

No doubt you are enraged. You might be sweating. This is the power of thought and the words we use to communicate with our emotions. You can't separate the two.

If these thoughts can take over and continue this way, they dig deep and build a lifelong resentment. We can hold onto our resentment for a very long time, as it slowly eats away at our life.

Now, think about something that makes you happy: working on a passion project; a childhood memory; or spending time with your friends, family, or children. You can feel your emotions shifting from rage to a happy, jovial feeling. Concentrate on these thoughts long enough, and you change your state for the long-term.

The ability to change your state of mind is the most powerful strategy you can implement today. The one reason people are so unhappy is because they are stuck in a state of mind that is controlling their emotions. They latch onto an idea or a negative thought that is all-encompassing, and it consumes them.

This is how people become agitated, depressed, or even suicidal. They can't break out of their negative thought patterns. They feel hopeless. Helpless. They have nothing to live for. Life becomes an exhausting loop and we just want it to stop. In many cases, people need help, intervention, or just someone to talk to about how they are feeling.

Your emotional state is always in your control. We can't stop people from acting, saying, or being the way that they are. They are running their own show, and it usually has nothing to do with you. But when people—whether they be family members, co-workers, or strangers—do something that affects our emotional state, we take it personally.

But remember this: Many people aren't aware of your feelings. How could they be? They are too focused on their own lives. Now, while there are people out there who take pleasure in hurting others emotionally, most people do it unintentionally believing they are right and can act, say, or be anyway they want to.

When we meet someone whose behavior we don't like, and they insult us or try to control us, our reaction is to resist. We want to fight back and put up our own barriers to defend our keep. This is the first step to building resentment. From here it can only get worse. You are now betting your emotional state on what the other person is going to do next.

Will they act against me? Derail me efforts or resort to bullying? Are they talking about me?

Your thoughts take off on a wild rampage and build up a wall of fear that snowballs into a giant mess by the end of the day. Stress, worry, and fear go hand-in-hand when we lose control over our thoughts and let go of the right to master our emotions.

There are several core strategies we can use to master our emotions at the basic level.

Meditation, focused thinking, or relaxing music can bring you back to the present moment. In fact, the only peace you can find is right now— in this moment.

Your thoughts will try to jump from now to tomorrow to weeks from now, creating scenarios that don't exist. But your mind doesn't know this. It isn't aware of what is real and what isn't.

What you think about all day long is what you become. We have heard this before, but when you are stuck in a real situation that requires you to step back and observe the problem, you can see how easily it is to get sucked down a negative hole.

If you want to master your emotional state, you will have to start with bringing your thoughts into the present moment. Calm down the screaming mind. Doesn't it feel like your mind is screaming at you sometimes? You want to shut it down, so you turn on the TV or listen to loud music. But that rarely helps. It just creates a distraction. As soon as the TV show is over, you are back to Square One.

What you need to do is to break the pattern. Engage your negative thinking and the screaming voices in your head. They are not running the show as we have been deceived into thinking. It is all you. It is your show, and you are the director of your own performance. So, stand up and take charge.

Disengage Your Negative Loop

You can disengage the thoughts that are running through your mind and creating patterns of negative chaos. When you are stuck in a negative mental loop, your mind is playing the same old tape repeatedly. Every time it runs through the scenario, it becomes stronger, adding more intensity to the images. You feel worse because you feel powerless to end it.

But your emotions and feelings are being built on the images playing in your mind. People who have been through trauma know this all too well. They play the same recording—real or imagined—in their minds until it becomes an all-consuming sensation. Imagine if you walked around all day, concentrating on the worst event of your life? How would you feel? You'd be anxious, fearful, and miserable.

> *"Realize that if a door closed, it's because what was behind it wasn't meant for you."*
>
> **— Mandy Hale**

Here is how we can change it: By changing the way that the story is written and replacing it with something better, we can break the negative-pattern loop and lay the foundation for something positive that feels good.

After all, isn't that what we want? To feel good about ourselves, our surroundings, and to see people in a different way even if their actions bring us pain? Up to now, you have been focused on the other person, and wishing, wanting, or hoping they would change their ways. But as I said, people are people. One day they are your friends and the next day, well, they are someone else. They have their own side of the street to clean and you have yours.

Imagine if you could change your emotional well-being at any moment. When you fall into a negative path, you can reach down and pull yourself out of it. When someone gets in your face and their attitude or actions are making you sweat with anger, you can calm your mind and manage your state in the worst of conditions. I know it sounds like a dream, but believe me, I have had great success—and failure—with this over the years.

In the study of neuroscience, we now know that our brain connects physical patterns to the habits we engage in regularly. So, if your habit is to get angry or lose your temper suddenly, that behavior is recorded, and it gets more powerful the more you exercise it.

Now, think about the thought patterns you have that are directly linked to your emotions. If you lock into the same pattern every day, multiple times per day, you are creating a powerful bond that becomes unbreakable. The only way to break it down is to stop the pattern of thought and begin by building a new one.

Step One: Catch the Trigger Thought or Image

This step involves catching your thoughts when they latch onto a negative idea. Think of it this way: When you watch the same movie again and again, the movie itself never changes. It is the same film every time. Our thoughts can act like the scenes of a movie, replaying without change and reinforcing limited beliefs with each replay.

Step Two: Cut the Limited Thought Pattern

Over the course of years, we buy into the limitations that define our actions. When you catch your thoughts that are playing the same movie reels over and over, then it's like taking a pair of scissors and cutting that film. When you find yourself trapped in a negative loop, visualize taking a set of scissors and cutting the film in two. This puts a stop to the internal ranting.

Step Three: Repeat this Process

If something works, try it again. Continue to practice it until you can shIft your emotions at will. Your emotions are powerful and make or break you.

By realizing how quickly you can change your own state, you add a new level of confidence to your personal mastery. You are no longer a victim to circumstances or other peoples' mood swings. You are not affected by another's bad day.

Practice these techniques, and you will cut off negative thought patterns before they have a chance to break into your mind and ruin your day.

Chapter 14

Develop the Habit of Intentional Thinking

"We cannot become what we need to be by remaining what we are."

— Max Depree

If you work on any habit, make the first one a habit to control your thoughts. This is one of the best habits you will ever develop—more so than time management or even eating habits.

Once you have the habit of feeding your thoughts the information you want them to have, the rest just falls into place. Consider your thinking as the central core to all else that is happening.

Thinking creates emotions. It creates responses and is responsible for the kingdom of your mind. People who thrive in a successful environment have arrived there because they have powerful thoughts that guide them every step of the way.

How many successful negative thinkers do you know? I don't know too many, but I know a lot of positive thinkers who work hard and believe that what they are doing is making a difference.

A person who has a positive mental attitude also has a pattern of strong positive thoughts. I know there are tons of books and material out there on why we need to maintain a positive attitude throughout life. The reasons are obvious. Negative thoughts are dangerous—just as dangerous as smoking or drinking heavily. In a way, negative thinking is also an addiction.

People fall into the pattern of reacting to a situation from a negative point of view and this becomes their default mindset. When you live this way, you'll attract like/negative people to engage with. Positive people who are upbeat and happy have no reason or interest to share time with people who bring them down.

Negative people are the same way. If they can't convert positive-minded people to join in their misery, they find someone who will listen. Like attracts like. You can have one side or the other but not both.

If your default habit is reacting negatively, that is okay. You can change this. It won't happen overnight, but if you maintain persistent focus and remember to force the habit to change, you will change it. Negative behavior is addictive and easy to fall into. Positive behavior is addictive, as well, but more difficult to maintain because of the work you have put in.

There are no advantages to having an NMA. You might be thinking "I already know that," but regardless, I see many people every day who have a big chip on their shoulder and they are looking for someone to unload all their misery on. There are also some people who think they are positive players, but in fact it is an illusion.

If you are unhappy, discontent, dissatisfied, live in fear, believe in limitations, or have a lot of anger and you don't know why, chances are you suffer from some form of a negative mental mindset. And if you do, that is okay. That is why we are here.

I believe too many people are slaves to their own vices. They think they have no choice in so many situations. However, it is just the opposite. It is not the situations we have to learn to adapt to; it is the power of our mind, and how it is trained to perceive its surroundings. You cannot control others (and you shouldn't), and if they try to control you, that is their choice. *They* will suffer for it.

Failing to develop your positive mindset is setting yourself up for failing in most other areas too. If you fall into the bad habit of not working on your attitude, you risk falling into a negative mindset. Remember this: You have two paths you can take. One path leads to forging strong relationships, quality lifestyle, and turning your thoughts into dreams.

The other path is the opposite and is the path unfortunately most people choose "unconsciously" when they lose touch with themselves. Believing in limitations, using words that demean or harm yourself and others, complaining and bickering, or reacting to your emotions without thinking is the way to suffering.

Do you like suffering? I don't know of anyone who does, and yet every day, people act out in ways that add to the suffering of either themselves or somebody else. The news is rife with it. Our communities are full of it. You can start with your own temple of success in your mind. Make a choice to be different, and you will be. By not making a choice, you choose the other path by default.

Your positive mindset is the foundation on top of what everything else is achieved. You can't build the home of your dreams on a faulty foundation.

Core Strategies for Creating a Positive Attitude

Here are two strategies for building and maintaining a positive attitude that, if practiced, will change the course of your life.

1. **Stay connected with your thoughts.** Observe what is happening with your thinking, and then start to make slight adjustments. This won't happen instantly. And even for people who are highly positive, creative, and successful, they, too, must stay frosty and be on top of things. A positive mental attitude is not a goal to achieve. It is a state of mind you must work your way into, and then maintain. Just as a garden is never truly rid of its weeds because new ones crop up every day, your mind needs constant attention, too.

2. **Pay attention.** When a negative thought creeps in, just let it happen. You can't combat everything, and you are going to have bad days when the world is garbage, and you wonder why you are here at all. It happens. When you have one of those "life is absolute garbage" days, let it be. It is also unrealistic to think you can be a loving, positive individual made of unstoppable success every day. You won't be, but if you train yourself to be like this most days, you will fare better in the end. Have your bad day, and then get back to it.

Go back through the book and jot down the ways to create a positive mindset. Gratitude, affirmations, and reading self-help books are just a few ways to reinforce your attitude of growth and to get rid of negative thinking. Just doing a few of the things on the list is going to make a big impact on your quality of life.

Here are additional suggestions for creating a PMA:

- Focus on what you love to do and start doing it.
- Leave your failures outside of your mind. Keep them as reminders and lessons learned but they are not your future.
- Get a mentor or accountability partner. Learn from this person and do what they have done.
- Make "Affirmation Repetition" a habit. Have a list of affirmations or quotes you can read at the start of every day. Check the back of this book for affirmation suggestions.
- Do one act of kindness at least once a day.
- Spend 30 minutes with your thoughts every evening. This means turning off all devices, the TV, and shutting yourself away for 30 minutes. This doesn't mean you have to meditate, but just be one with your thoughts.
- Check your Anger Meter every now and then. I have a confession to make. I have an anger streak in me. One negative thought leads to another and within no time I am angry, resentful, and full of negativity. It became a massive spiral that sucks me down into a black pit of ooze. Not much fun. I wouldn't recommend it.

Recognizing that you are angry and building up to an attack is the first big step. Talking yourself down is the next thing you can do.

- A defeat is not a loss; life is not all a streak of wins. You will stumble and fall. Get back up and try it again. Persistence is a major positive skill that is going to give you a huge PMA if you keep it up.
- Write down one thing you are grateful for every day. Do this as soon as you wake up. It will take 10 seconds. Just one thing. Keep a gratitude list. I started to keep one two years ago. I write down one thing every morning or at night that I am grateful for.
- Don't rely on things for your happiness or fulfillment.
- Nobody can make you feel miserable or sad; that is a choice.
- Avoid making time for people who like to waste yours.
- Believe that freedom is your choice; you can either free your mind or keep it enslaved with negative thoughts and images. Would you rather be free or be a slave to your alternative self?

What lessons have you learned? You can add them to this list to remind you of what you can do and to see how far you have come. Now that we have the essential elements to create your attitude, what are you going to do with it?

Chapter 15

Destroy Your Distractions

"One way to boost our will power and focus is to manage our distractions instead of letting them manage us."

— Daniel Goldma

W e all have a "Monkey Mind"—a term coined by Buddha that suggests that within each of us, there are a gang of monkeys wreaking havoc on our thoughts.

Your Monkey Mind is very active most of the time, with your thoughts competing for attention. From this mind full of chaos, we are interrupted by fear, inattention, and, at times, harsh criticism. This criticism is often directed toward us as negative self-talk.

One of the greatest challenges we deal with daily is taming the Monkey Mind inside our own minds.

The End of Monkey Mind

The daily distractions we are challenged to deal with all stem from the Monkey Mind. As we already looked at in Part I, mindfulness is the path to creating a calm, peaceful mind. You will never be rid of the chaos of your own thinking; that is not what this is about. But better yet, you are learning the right way to master your thoughts and calm the chaos of thoughts that are running the show.

Can you imagine where you would be if you could turn off the distractions that pull you away from your goals and true purpose in life? What could you achieve? Who would you become?

Raising awareness of the things that distract you goes a long way to becoming more productive and less chaotic. This consistent pattern of being distracted and chasing white rabbits down multiple paths has a negative effect on our thoughts. If you are constantly battling the distractions in your world—and we all are—it consumes your energy and you end up feeling exhausted by the end of the day.

Monkey Mind is the result of our thoughts being scattered to the wind. Ever see leaves blow around in autumn after dropping from the tree? That is what our thoughts look like when we get caught up in Monkey Mind thinking. There is very little rhyme or reason. But there is a system we can put in place right now to stop our mind from running away.

The problem is not that we are easily distracted. There will always be something to pull our thoughts away from what we intend to do. The real issue is with your own mind. You have to train your thoughts to stay fixed in the moment and on the task that it is working on. This can be done by conditioning your mind to stay fixed on its true purpose.

But first of all, what is distracting you? As one of the attendees in my workshop responded, "The question is what *doesn't* distract me?"

When we are overwhelmed and burdened by the need to respond to everything, and we treat each issue as urgent, we lose the essence of priority. How can we calm our thinking and gain greater control over our own minds when it feels like giants are trying to break down our mental barriers?

In a workshop I joined years ago, one of the speakers had asked the audience what they think about while brushing their teeth. Everyone had to write down at least one thought they had while brushing their teeth. People had tons of things they would work on mentally while scrubbing away at their whites.

Here are some examples:

- *Helping my children with their homework*
- *Taking out the garbage*
- *Preparing a report for tomorrow*
- *How to talk to my husband about our finances*
- *Getting ready for vacation next month*
- *What will I do on my next day off?*
- *What will happen if...?*

Only one of the participants had written down: "*I think about my teeth.*"

The Monkey Mind is always active, and it likes to keep busy. As we are working on one task, our mind is already planning another. It's like preparing for a turkey dinner, and you have 10 things in the oven all at once, and they all need attention *right now!*

When we don't get a grip on what is distracting us, we fail to get the most important stuff done because everything is competing for attention. Goals go unachieved, cleaning doesn't get done, and application forms that should have been filled out are still lying around months later. Distraction breeds fearful thinking because we believe we should be somewhere else doing something else so that we can feel more productive.

It comes down to simplifying your mind. Put an end to the hamster wheel, or, at the very least, slow it down so we can catch our breath. Let's give those hamsters a break!

This brings us to the power of living in the present moment. We know what the present moment is. It is what meditators talk about when they get into deep meditation. Staying in one place, enjoying the moment, and letting go of your thoughts. Mindfulness is simply observing what you are thinking about in the present moment.

Do you know why this matters? First of all, fear is strongest when it is focused on the future. This is where our worry spends most of its time. The big, "What if...?" question comes to life. Monkey Mind loves to focus on future events. Most importantly, it fixes on the endgame of what will happen. Scarcity over not having enough money, losing loved ones, a pet dying, or the economy collapsing.

I can cut through the suspense and tell you how many of these events will happen someday: All of them. If you live long enough, you'll go through loss, suffering, good times, and bad times. Haven't you already been experiencing this?

The future will be no different than the past has been. Once we come to accept this, we can stop worrying and calm the Monkey Mind way of thinking down. Or better yet, silence it for good.

> "One way to boost our will power and focus is to manage our distractions instead of letting them manage us."
>
> — Virat Kohli

Overcoming the habit of distraction is not about controlling your social-media activity or limiting the amount of time you spend watching television. What it really comes down to is focusing on why we are distracted. When you observe your own mind in action, and the activity going on, you can see what pulls you in.

You are distracted by chaos because you have conditioned yourself to chase shiny objects. The problem is not the object itself. It is our reaction to the object when it suddenly appears.

The focused mind, trained to concentrate, can ignore the first thought that it has and is able to manage the chaos going on around it. If you want to master your thoughts and be less distracted by chaos, it starts with observing your impulse reactions.

This brings us to the key to reducing your need to be distracted: **The Distraction Trigger.**

Identify Your Triggers

Your mind works differently than anyone else's, and because of that, you need to identify what distracts you. Most of our so-called distractions are really just bad habits. Think about it for a minute: checking your email fifty times a day has nothing to do with checking email. It is an addictive habit that you have created. So, to break it, you need to recognize when you are reacting to your urge/need to fulfill your instant gratification.

What happens the moment you react when you get an email? Your favorite gossiper calls you to tell you about their day? The TV magically turns on and you start watching old reruns of *Little House on the Prairie* again instead of writing that book or working on your online business?

In most cases, we are distracted or procrastinate because we want to be. Here are excuses we use to stay in distraction mode that invariably leads to procrastination:

- *If I watch TV for 30 minutes, I'll just be able to relax more before I work out.*
- *I should respond to this text message right now because XXXX is probably waiting on the other end. Besides, I have already read it, and she knows that.*
- *I'll do it tomorrow because I'll feel more energetic.*

And on it goes...

Your mind is a restless machine. It looks to keep busy and this is a good thing. But without something to focus on, boredom sets in and the need to alleviate that boredom and restlessness gets stronger.

If you've ever tried to resist something you know that the more you try, the harder it gets. A snack? Watching TV? Starting a new habit? Checking email?

Your mind, and similarly your thinking, is hardwired to respond to stimuli. Your stimulant is different from mine but we both have our triggers that set us off.

My random, impulsive action was turning on the TV—even if I was in the middle of something else. Then, 30 minutes would pass, and when I tried to get back into what I had been doing, I had lost momentum. My thoughts at this point were stimulated again, and now, since I'd already killed an hour watching television, why not check my email, too? The spiral began, and from there, you can imagine I wasn't getting much done.

Now, make a list of the triggers that set you up for failure. How can you break that trigger by removing the mechanism? For example, I would unplug the TV during the week and put the remote away. When it came to checking my email every 10 minutes, I removed the open tab on my browser because every time I scrolled by it, I'd check email. When I would get distracted by a sugar craving, I started keeping fruit nearby, instead of a drawer full of snacks.

Identify your trigger and prepare to tackle it before it happens. When you do get hit with a need to react, you can find a healthier alternative. Boredom can be replaced with reading a book. Do you know why most people are addicted to smartphones these days? They found instant pleasure that removes the feeling of boredom they experience.

In fact, boredom is the single biggest reason we lean toward addictions and compulsive habits. Why be bored when you can be stimulated? But after the stimulation wears off, how do you feel? Relieved for a brief time. Then, the cycle picks up again.

I have the Kindle app on all my devices, including my phone. When the urge to check email or social media hits me, I can swipe open the app and start reading a book instead. This is a better alternative to counting likes on Facebook.

When it comes to your devices, either your phone or tablet, remove the apps that are junk. You don't need social media on your phone. I removed all of that and since then, I spend less time flipping and swiping and looking for something to empower my confidence. My empowerment now comes from knowing that I can control these impulses.

Check your emotions and tune in to how you are feeling. When you are irritable, moody, or restless, this is the prime time to escape. So, the question is, what should we run to?

Procrastination Is a Big Monkey

If you are easily distracted, this could be a set up for breeding the habit of procrastination. Realize that it isn't that you are being distracted by your environment. You are looking for a reason to be distracted.

Your need and desire to procrastinate is a big monkey that is looking for any and all reasons to drift away from the tasks that you should be doing. Your thoughts are searching for something to get stimulated.

If you have something that needs to be done, but you don't want to do it, you'll find something to distract you away from the task.

This is why you need to...

Work on a Specific Goal

We covered goal setting in the section on focus, but just in case you need a reminder: **Setting goal-specific tasks will keep you on track.** People with clear goals that they are excited about are less distracted and more motivated to stay on course. The Monkey Mind doesn't deal well with goals. It prefers the chaos of multitasking and the all-consuming preoccupation of the mind to stick around. But we want Monkey Mind to take a walk.

At the start of each day, set three specific goals. It can be something as simple as reading 10 pages of your book of the week. But be specific on your goals.

For example, my goals for today are:

1. Write 1000 words for my next book;
2. 2. Do a 20-minute workout with a medicine ball; and
3. Email three people for a guest post interview.

A restless mind can lead to boredom and looking around for something to entertain you. Having a specific goal to work toward builds the focus habit and blocks out those distractions. Remember: We allow ourselves to invite distractions in when feeling bored or restless.

> *"Procrastination is the bad habit of putting off until the day after tomorrow what should have been done the day before yesterday."*
>
> **— Napoleon Hill**

Your goals will keep you on track. Set three goals a day. If this feels too much, set just one. But remember, having nothing to focus on leaves you open to doing anything when you have free time.

Did you know that over 90 percent of the people you see every day do not have any goals for themselves? Is it any wonder they are looking for something to keep their minds busy? A lack of goals leads to feelings of despair, worry. Without a goal to focus on, your thoughts latch onto the weaker links such as distractions that lead to procrastination.

Your goals could consist of:

- Exploring a new business idea that you came up with;
- Walking 10,000 steps a day;
- Creating new recipes or practicing a recipe you discovered;
- Setting up a financial plan for your family;
- Taking a series of online courses to expand your tech knowledge; and/or
- Writing a book or working on a blog post.

Block Your Time in 15-Minute Increments

Time is a valuable resource. It's more valuable than money because it cannot be replaced. Once your time is gone; it's gone forever. Who has time to waste in mind-numbing tasks when we could be doing what we love? But it isn't that easy when there is so much to do at once.

Monkey Mind lives for this. It wants you to multitask and do as much or as little as you can. This is why I started breaking my time into small chunks—15-minute chunks, to be exact.

Why 15 minutes?

Well, it reduces that overwhelming feeling of overcommitting to something big. Have you ever told yourself, "Today I'm going to work on (choose activity here) for three hours," only in the end you did much less than expected? It is hard to concentrate, as we already know. Start small.

Go for the lowest-common denominator. You can do anything for 15 minutes, right? You can even sit in stillness and think about your thoughts.

Use a timer and set it for 15 minutes. Decide what you are going to work on for 15 minutes.

Will you:

- Meditate?
- Start writing a blog post?
- Send an email that you've been putting off?
- Listen to a piece of classical music?

The purpose is to discipline your mind to stick with a habit. In this case, a habit of working within a short amount of time. By limiting this habit to just 15 minutes, you are not overcommitting or stressing out about not acting.

Focus on Just One Task

Multitasking doesn't work, and you are no more productive when working on several things at the same time. To be really effective, your mind can accomplish anything if it focuses on just one task at a time.

If you are working on a project that has multiple steps and will take several months to complete, break it down into sub-steps and mini actions.

Plan your actions ahead and know what you are working on, and then commit to this one action for the allocated time.

Be Aware of Your Anxiety

One reason we get distracted is because we lose touch with our emotional program. When you feel bored, you want to be entertained. When you are feeling fearful, you would rather be distracted in order to deal with the fear.

Anxiety creates fearful thinking. And, if you are a nervous or fearful person, you have more anxiety than others. When I get anxious, I get restless and bored. I look for something to fix me and this could lead to poor choices. When this happens, you can calm yourself down by listening to a favorite piece of music or practice deep breathing. I would recommend NOT turning on the TV or using the computer during your times of anxiety.

Mind-numbing activities will help you escape, but those same emotions are still there looking for some stillness to their existence. Mastering your emotions is an amazing form of self-control.

Learning to direct your actions and not just doing something habitually will put you in greater control of your own life and choices.

I recommend that you:

1. Read a part from a book. Try *Stillness Speaks* by Eckhart Tolle or *Fear: Essential Wisdom for Getting Through the Storm* by Thich Nhat Hanh.
2. For music, check out "Weightless" by Marconi Union. This song is considered to be one of the most relaxing songs in the world. It has done wonders for my anxiety moments.
3. Meditate. Just put yourself in a place of quiet calmness and use the 15-minute-block technique. Play a song while meditating and relax. If you need some suggestions for meditation, check out *Meditation for Beginners: 20 Practical Tips for Understanding the Mind* by Leo Babauta.
4. Read positive quotes and affirmations to yourself. Yes, quotes are powerful enough to put your mind in a relaxed state. They can raise your energy level and put your mind in a positive state.

Start Keeping a Goals Journal

I've talked about the importance of goals several times in this book, so you know how serious I am about creating a goal. Keeping a goals journal is a great first step.

This is a journal for keeping track of the goals you are working on, notes about progress, and challenges along the way. You can fill up your journal with positive quotes and affirmations as well.

At the end of the day, spend a few minutes reading through your journal. Prioritize the mini tasks you are working on, so you will know that you are working on something. Create a checklist of your goals and set up daily tasks. Schedule time every morning or evening to write something in your journal.

I added a new goal every day—even if it was a small one. After six months, I had over 200 written down. If you want to distract your mind, divert your attention toward setting and working toward these goals.

Chapter 16

Retrain Your Brain

> *"In order to carry a positive action, we must develop here a positive vision."*
>
> **— Dalai Lama**

As we've learned, our thoughts have a direct influence on the way we live. Our quality of life can be traced back to the quality of our own thoughts. But how often do you find yourself trapped in a negative thought-loop that just spins on forever? How much mental energy is spent on replaying the old tapes from your past and listening to the critical voices that feel like they are running the show?

Eliminate Negative Thinking and Take Control of Your Thoughts

Just as a positive mindset fills you up with creative energy, your negative mindset, and the negative thoughts that go with it, deplete your mental and physical energy. You feel lethargic. You get headaches more frequently. You are less motivated to work, play, or interact with anyone.

The core of your focus is on what you don't like, who you resent, what you don't have, and how bad life has turned out for you. Negative thinking is poison for your mind.

Your mission: Eliminate this crap.

But it isn't just your mind that is affected. Your physiology is influenced, as well. Negative thoughts make you sick more often, and because you think you are depressed, you take medication. Only instead of helping you to overcome the real core issues, you stay depressed and continue to live in a world of negativity.

In most cases, it is not our environment that needs to change. It isn't the other people that have to shape up and treat you better. You don't have to hope for things to get better, because they won't. You *make* things better by deciding to transform your thoughts.

Negative thoughts—just like positive ones—don't happen by pure chance. We create our own misery, just the same as we create our own happiness. Surprisingly, many people believe that happiness is what happens when things work out perfectly, or when we finally get everything we want in life.

Until then, we stay neutral or miserable, struggling through our days, hoping for the best. Negative thoughts thrive in this environment. Your negative persona is searching for a reason to exist. When you focus on what you don't have, how bad the economy is, or the bad situation you are in, you open the door for your negative thoughts to take over.

Here is what S.J. Scott says about negative thoughts, from his book *Declutter Your Mind* with Barrie Davenport:

> *"Many people go through their entire lives victimized by their negative thoughts. They feel they have no control of what thoughts take up residence in their brains—and worse, they believe the 'voices' in their heads that tell them the sky is falling."*

Though it may feel natural to allow your mind to wander into worry and despair, you're reinforcing negative thinking by not challenging it and by accepting your thoughts as your identity. But you have the power to recognize this tendency and change it by building the reframing habit.

From now on, I want you to picture negative thoughts as intruders, taking up space in your head. If they stay there, you will continue to repeat past failures. Knock each of these intruders out of your mind as they pop up.

If you don't do this, you will fail to achieve your goals and every action you take will feel like an uphill battle. Negative thinking is powerful but remember: You are responsible for feeding into it. You create your own thoughts—good or bad.

What happens when we build negative thoughts into our thought paradigm? The world becomes a dark, painful existence. For me, suffering is when I let the demons of negativity take over and run my emotions.

When you are stuck in a negative frame of mind, and you think there is no way out, you will stop looking for the exit. I don't know of anyone who purposefully *wants* to suffer.

Yet, our negative thinking is just that: a form of self-destruction. For many people, we go through days—and even weeks—in which things are not going right. Negative thoughts can be triggered by a crisis in your family, a trauma at work, a painful breakup, or financial burden. Life is not fair, but then again, what *is* fair? When everything works out perfectly, and we get everything we want without having to work for it?

"Life isn't fair." This is a statement to the universe that says, "I am a victim in this life, and I deserve better." The people who deserve better are the people who *make it better*. Sitting around, waiting for change, is the same as expecting to win the lottery when you don't even buy lottery tickets.

Let's look at how you can retrain your brain to think differently. You are never too old, too educated, or too good for leveling up your mind and ridding yourself of the negative influences that have planted their flag in your mind.

Picture this as a new garden that you worked hard to plant and grow your seeds. The next day, the garden is corrupted by weeds. Would you walk away and let them grow, destroying all your work? Of course not.

As **James Allen** said:

> *"A person sooner or later discovers that he or she is the master-gardener of their soul, the director of his or her own life."*

You are the master-gardener, and this is your life. It doesn't obey circumstances, and you are not stuck doing anything you don't want to do. Your thoughts—and the actions you take that are driven by thought—build your tomorrow. You will always follow through on what your mind is telling you to do. But who is giving the commands?

You are.

Let's look at how you and I are influenced by the random thoughts that just pop up and start ruining everything. Most of your thoughts are so normal (to you) that you likely don't even question them. But these are the areas of our thinking we need to pay attention to the most. It is what we accept as "natural" that is the hardest to change because we can't always see it.

Sometime others may be point it out. They might say, "Hey, you are really rude sometimes," or worse. But if we fail to even recognize it, we will refute the claim and continue to act like a jerk. Imagine if you could alter just one pathway in your mind. What could you achieve?

After all, this is what mental roadblocks are: obstacles that stick because we don't have the tools to remove them.

But we do now. You have this book, and the corresponding material to go with it, so change it, you can—and you will! Nothing is impossible—unless your thoughts tell you it is. But that doesn't make it true.

Now, let's dive into the strategies for retraining your brain to recognize your negative thoughts and free your mental blocks. Then, you will know a freedom like nothing else.

The Danger of Negative Thinking

We know negative thinking is not healthy. It's not like we wake up every morning and decide to make it the worst day we've ever had. But that is what happens to millions of people every day. They move through life, listening to the toxic voices inside, believing the criticisms and fearful thoughts provoking us to worry and feel anxious.

Where do you think worry comes from? Worry is a result of being fearful of the future. Anxiety has a strong part to play in your past. You know you can't change anything from what has been said and done, so you linger back there, trying to sort out what happened, replaying angry conversations, and hanging on to old resentments.

Our thoughts are dangerous if we let them run loose. We end up sabotaging what could be glorious moments and destroying memories in a moment. Think about this: **Your emotions will always follow your thoughts.**

Imagine going through life angry. Every day, you are pissed-off, fearful, and frightened. Now, take it a step further. Because you're always angry, you take it out on your family or a pet. When they do something that annoys you, how do you react? In anger. Your negative, angry thoughts are not only damaging your own mind.

You can exercise that power in the world by bringing it out into the open. Soon the people who are around you disappear. They remember you as that person who was always in a bad mood. What creates a mood? The thoughts you have been dwelling on all week.

Recognize your negative thoughts, change them day by day, and gradually your life becomes a better memory. You will draw people to you instead of scaring them away. Remember that your external reality will always reflect your internal thought processes. What you think about all day long is who you become.

It is such an easy concept. People think they need to figure everything out and get to the root of the problem. So, what do they do? They expect the other person to change so they can feel better. Haven't you ever said to yourself: "I wouldn't feel this way if he would just...."

The world and the people in it do not owe you anything. Nobody will recognize that they are in the wrong even if you point it out to them. It is up to you to find meaning in your own thinking patterns and look to change it. And by change it I mean, transform your thoughts. I know, easier said than done, right? But not impossible. People change every day. It may take months to see results, but it starts now.

To recap, negative thinking does the following:

- Sabotages your future;
- Destroys potentially good memories;
- Ruins your physical and mental health;
- Creates anger that sabotages relationships;
- Increases the chances of depression;
- Makes us restless and irritable; and
- Creates feelings of desperation.

Remove Negative Phrases That Keep You Stuck

How many negative phrases can you count in a day? I'll bet you have as many as I do, and I can catch myself on many of them. But what makes these negative connotations stick is that we justify being used or abused.

- "If only he/she would stop…."
- "I can't believe they did that. Now I'm screwed."
- "Nothing ever works out for me. I told you so."
- "He makes me so angry."
- "Everything would be so perfect if only…."
- "All I want is (fill in your desire here) and then I'll be happy."
- "See how much she has, and look at how little I have?"
- "Life just isn't fair."
- "Some people have all the luck."

By playing the victim, you place yourself in a position of power. You want to be right and they are wrong. You want to be understood while the misunderstanding lies with the other person. You want an apology for being wronged so you can justify how right you always are.

Here is what I do. Carry a small notebook with you. You can use a tablet, but I prefer actual paper because digital material gets lost easily. Throughout the day, when you start to complain or use one of your negative phrases, write it down. Right there. This will make you aware of what you are thinking and saying that keeps your self-pity train moving.

Self-pity is another form of negative thought. It spins a web of lies that tell us, "If I am the victim, I don't have to do anything." Use your notebook to identify the phrases you use. Then, add up the phrases you have most commonly used. Everybody has several that they love to use repeatedly.

Disempower Your Inner Voice

We all have a big, loud inner voice. You can hear this voice clearly when you try something new, when you fail, or when you are feeling afraid. It is the voice of self-sabotage, and it is not too kind. This voice is your mind is feeding you lies, and it always has. It is strong because you have listened to it for so long, it sounds normal.

To quiet this voice, you must replace it with another voice—your true voice. This is the voice of compassion. It is the voice you were born with and not the tormented demon that runs lose inside your head, trying to create havoc.

When your thoughts are in such a disorganized array, it seems you have little to no control over them. But that isn't true. You can stop the roller coaster of disempowering thoughts anytime. You have the power to throw the switch and put an end to your inner critic. It may take a lot of attempts but, every time it speaks up, shut it down.

Recognize Who and What Triggers Negative Thoughts.

Most of your negative thinking is attached to something—a person, place or situation—that acts as a trigger. If it is a person, they could be your spouse, neighbor, or co-worker/manager. Sometimes, all it takes is one thought about this person to send you on a negative tangent in your mind that could derail your entire day.

By focusing on the object of your anger and resentment, you are feeding the negative energy that keeps it alive. You can blame, criticize, and condemn as much as you like, but the only one that suffers is yourself.

> *"Your mind is the basis of everything you experience and of every contribution you make to the lives of others. Given this fact, it makes sense to train it."*
>
> **— Sam Harris**

I know one man who was fired from his job over a misunderstanding with his employer. For months, he was angry. When he drove past the building the company was located in, he became hostile and violent and developed a deep resentment. What was triggering this? He was deliberately driving past the building and setting off his negative energy. Once he recognized this trigger and quit this destructive habit, the negative thoughts were gradually replaced with a better outlook that focused on getting a better job.

You could be hung up on a breakup, harboring a resentment toward your parents, or focusing on ways to get back at someone for injuring you emotionally or financially. Triggers set us up for failure and drag us into the depths of negative bias. We can conjure up all sorts of reasons to hold onto our resentments. But the only thing we will succeed at doing is feeding into our own misery.

Take note of what your trigger is, whether it is a person or place, and start removing these thoughts from your mind.

Here is one idea: Try the rubber-band trick. Place 5-10 rubber bands on your wrist. When you get stuck on a negative thought, take one of the bands and move it to your other wrist. This is a great visual aid to show you just how many negative thoughts you have, and how much progress you are making to crush those thoughts.

Stay Engaged with Positive Action

Staying engaged in a project or a hobby that you are passion about keeps negative thinking out of your head. It is hard to let bad thoughts grow when you are happy and working on something that has meaning to you.

Examples of this are:

- Studying another language
- Learning to play a musical instrument
- Listening to inspiring music
- Writing a book
- Creating a business plan
- Working on repairs for your house
- Reading a book
- Working on your goals

Taking positive action is the best way to stay engaged and when your mind is occupied with a creative activity, negative thinking has less chance of occupying your mental space.

Identify Your Common Worries

Everyone worries about something. In fact, it is nearly impossible to remove the habit of worrying. The best you can do is reduce the amount of time you spend worrying.

Do you know which area of your life you worry about the most? We all have things that cause us stress, and when this happens, our thoughts latch onto the uncertainty of the future. Do you worry about:

- Having enough money for retirement;
- Your child's future;
- Someone's plans to build a high-rise in your quiet neighborhood
- The next election?

While most of our worries are fleeting and last just a few minutes, it is your chronic, repetitive worries you want to zero in on. How many times a day do worrisome thoughts cross your mind about lack of money? Does this keep you awake late at night? Do you feel short of breath or panicked if you think about how little you have? Does this cause you to react aggressively?

Worry is a form of habitual thinking that sets us up for failure. You can't be caught up in thoughts of worry and have a peaceful mind at the same time. The way to eliminate the chronic worry habit is to act on the thing that worries you.

Are you afraid of not having money? Get educated on financial planning and set up a savings plan.

Kids' future? Talk with your kids about what they want to do. But remember: You are worrying about something you have no control over. Worrying about the future is pointless. It is a gray zone in which anything can happen.

Stay centered in the present moment and worrisome thoughts will not follow you there.

Put an End to Labeling

How many times a day do you label things as good, bad, or ugly? Here are some examples:

- "She's a real..."
- "I can't stand that guy. He's such a..."

You know how it goes. We condemn, judge, and assassinate the character of other people. We've all done it. Some people do it every day. For others, it is a habit that destroys their mindset. Yes, labeling is the #1 most destructive form of negativity you can practice. You tear down the reputation of others, while falsely building your own.

If you want to be free of negativity, the labeling must end. I don't mean just cut it in half—*get rid of it.*

But what about when someone makes me angry? Or insults me? Or they do something like rip me off or cut me off in traffic?

You're right. People act in disrespectful, arrogant, malicious ways all the time. Welcome to the real world. Not everybody plays nice. But will you throw away your mental toughness by lowering yourself to the act of labeling.

Calling someone out on their actions is a better way to approach this than labeling them for an action they have taken. Remember that peoples' behavior doesn't always reflect their true character. People make mistakes, do things out of character, and react toward a situation based on their experiences.

"Successful people maintain a positive focus in life no matter what is going on around them. They stay focused on their past successes rather than their past failures, and on the next action steps they need to take to get them closer to the fulfillment of their goals rather than all the other distractions that life presents to them."

— Jack Canfield,
bestselling author of *The Success Principles*

PART IV

The Four Pillars of
Strategic Thinking

Chapter 17

Pillar One:
Focused Concentration
and Channeling Flow

> *"The greatest force is derived from the power of thought. The finer the element, the more powerful it is. The silent power of thought influences people even at a distance, because mind is one as well as many. The universe is a cobweb; minds are spiders."*
>
> **— Swami Vivekananda**

In the previous section, we covered three critical areas. We learned that we can retrain our brains and eliminate the negative thinking that is corrupting our minds. We can do this by focusing on the positive forces in our lives and, deciding not to give into the weaker pull of the mind when it is drawn toward those negative objects.

You learned that the internal communication you have with yourself is really your mind trying to communicate with your thoughts, feelings, and emotions. This internal conversation is either positive or negative, depending on the information you are feeding it.

Most importantly, we know that our daily life is filled with distractions pulling us off course. Not just the obvious such as ping notifications or someone yelling, but the not-so-obvious internal factors we often neglect. We rarely acknowledge our own distracting thoughts swimming around, looking for something to target and direct energy toward.

This energy can be harnessed and controlled by two things: *Concentration* and *Flow.*

Empowering Your Concentration and Channeling Flow

Concentration is the ability to direct your thoughts with *intentional purpose.* It is the internal habit of focusing your mind on a specific task or goal until you have finished it. To take this a step further, it isn't just about accomplishing a goal. Rather, you are directing your thoughts to stay fixed on a task—not for reward or accomplishment but simply because you love doing it.

Concentration is the decision to direct your thoughts with intentional *force.* Your thoughts become creative energy when they are put to intentional work—regardless if the action brings about a good result. Your ability to concentrate is the same as being able to harness your attention and aim it toward your desire with a laser-focus.

Imagine yourself standing on the lakeshore and throwing a handful of rocks into the water. They spray out in all directions without any real intent. Then, you pick up a flat rock and skim it across the water. It moves rapidly in one direction and you have a much better chance of hitting your target.

This is how you want your thoughts to be: Focused in on one single task, committed to achieving your one objective. By concentrating your energy and pushing it into a funnel-like state, you are now harnessing the raw energy of your mind. It becomes a guiding force that enables you to build a business, create a purpose, or boost your productivity by 10 times just through focusing this attention and disengaging your distractions.

Many people I know are either engaged fully in feeding their distractions or, they are too busy trying to fight them off, invariably losing because they are too focused on winning the battle and not the war. If you are focusing your attention on your distractions, even without intention, you could be feeding them more power.

Most of the times, when we try to stop a behavior by focusing on that behavior, we end up with the opposite result. To change anything, you should fix your attention on the remedy. For example, by concentrating your mind energy on reducing negative thoughts, you don't think about your negative thoughts but rather, concentrate on the positive affirmations to remove them.

You can do something right now by acting on the remedy to heal those areas of yourself that are weakest. Many people, when they want to change, are too intent on the object they want to change.

Let's say you smoke, and you want to quit. You desperately want this habit to end. A lot of people walk around thinking, "I want to quit smoking; I want to quit smoking." But this just makes you want to indulge more. Instead, focus on what you want to *start* doing that will eliminate the bad habit.

Instead of saying to yourself, "I want to quit smoking," try, "I am exercising every day and eating healthy foods."

The shift to put an end to smoking will increase based on the actions taken toward this positive approach. In most cases, it isn't that we should stop doing things that are sabotaging us. But rather, we need to focus our attention on the behaviors we should *start* doing and *continue* to do.

Remember that you don't just follow through once and expect everything to change overnight. Like the athlete who runs the track each day, make your positive actions affirmative choices by deciding to practice it regularly.

If you can focus your thinking and direct your thoughts with intentional purpose toward something you are extremely passionate about, you break up all false limitations holding you back.

In fact, once you train your mind and direct those thoughts toward the focus of your deepest desires, you come to realize four critical points:

1. The only limitations you have are the limits of your thinking. As you expand and deepen your level of thought, your limitations melt away. You become limitless in your strategies.

2. Excuses you once made no longer make any sense. You stop making excuses and start creating real action steps that drive your forward.

3. The longer and more intensely you concentrate on a new behavior, the easier it becomes. By building a new habit that is resistant to the old behavior, you avoid falling back into old temptations. But, if you stop concentrating, your mind grows weak again and you slip back into old habits.

4. The focus of your concentration, whether it be reading a book or working on a new business, becomes your reality. You will always become what you focus on.

Focus on love and sending that out into the world, and you will receive love back. If you are anger-focused, and you concentrate on building up resentment, this is what will come back to you.

Concentration is a matter of streamlining your focus. It means to train your mind to concentrate fully on the task at hand, not because you have to, but because it is the only thing you want to do. Instead of your thoughts flying around haphazardly like leaves in the wind, you train your mind to stay fixed on its true purpose.

Your passion for a particular project or a hobby is the key to concentration. Your level of intensity is dependent on the strength of passion and drive you have for your goal.

Concentration turns confusion into clarity, and misdirection becomes a clear line of sight as you work with passion, intrinsic motivation, and full engagement. This can be a hobby you love or a dream that you are working toward. People who succeed in doing what they love can attribute this to their ability to stay centered on what they are doing through a state of flow.

You block the world away as you lose yourself.

"The secret of concentration is the secret of self-discovery. You reach inside yourself to discover your personal resources, and what it takes to match them to the challenge."

— Arnold Palmer

Empowering your concentration is about mastering your thoughts, actions, and habits. When you can redirect your thinking into taking the right actions, it naturally builds a bridge to habit development. When new habits are formed, if they are the right habits, they will work miracles for you. If they are the wrong habits, you will have a different experience.

Your ability to succeed or fail is dependent on your ability to isolate your concentration and focus on a particular subject over a length of time.

But the question is: "How much time?"

Concentrating is hard work, and you can easily get distracted. To be more successful, start with a smaller goal.

Fix your mind on something for just five minutes. Discipline your mind to stay with your point of focus. Then, concentrate on this one thing for five minutes. Every time you can focus for this duration, move the time ahead by another five minutes. Work your way up to 30 minutes. Then, try for 45 minutes, and, over time, stretch it to one hour. This won't be easy. It might take you months to build up this level of focused concentration.

But, what else are you going to do with your time? What goals are you trying to accomplish? I guarantee whatever it is, the reason you are not doing it is you are concentrating on other forces outside of yourself at a subconscious level. Everyone does this and we are so absorbed in our mental habits that we don't always see it.

Action Task: Concentration by Intention

Stay seated for 20 minutes and fix your mind on something you have always wanted. By selecting a goal or concentrating on a task at hand, you can move your thoughts in a position to succeed. Just like in sports, when we need our players to perform their best in their positions to win the game, we need to clearly state our objectives. Then, we need a game plan.

Your ability to stay fixed on one task is the key to mastering your own mind. When you can concentrate on the present moment, it releases you from the suffering of the past. It stops you from living in the anxiety of the unknown future. Now you can create your own future by living a life built by design and not just chance. How great is that?

To make this work in your favor and create the kind of life you intend to live, you need to create a clear, well-defined vision of what that would look like. What are you doing? How do you spend every day? Who are you with? Most importantly, how do you feel now that you are in this place?

Now that you have this image of what your future looks like, concentrate all your thoughts on making it happen. When self-doubt comes up—and it will—push it out of the way. Doubt is just your own mind playing games. Nobody can cast doubt on you. We do it to ourselves.

When you feel yourself being tempted by cravings and habits that want to steal your progress and potential, you can say no. You can choose not to act by concentrating your willpower on making clear choices.

Now that you have a clear mental picture of what you desire, who do you have in your life to help you build it? Who are the people you are spending your time with? At what degree are these people impacting your life in a positive way? Visualize the kind of people you need on your team, or individually, you may want a mentor or role model.

Next, **concentrate on the actions you are taking each day**. Are these actions in line with your goals? Are they moving you toward the results you need?

Right actions produce good results. The wrong actions, even with the best of intentions, can fail if we lose our focus for why we are doing this in the first place. This is why flow, which we will discuss in the next section, can put you into a state where all you think about is the task at hand.

In this state, nothing else matters. You are so passionate about this one thing that you can block out all other distractions. You are flowing through a positive state and your creativity is intense.

Use your affirmations, quotes, positivity tapes, or relaxing music. You can end your negative state at any time. What keeps it going and prolongs your suffering is...your own mind. And you are learning to master that through focus and concentrating on what matters most.

Concentration: A Form of Organized Energy

As soon as you are aware of your thoughts, and you can design your thinking at will, you now have the willpower to attract everything toward you. The concept is really simple. When we think of the law of attraction, we believe that what we wish for comes our way. But it has nothing to do with wishing. In fact, I am suggesting you ask the universe for nothing.

This concept goes against all the books out there on abundance, and how the universe is set up to deliver anything you want at any time. Well, it's not a fast-food restaurant. When you want something in this world, you don't wish for it—you work for it. The only way to work for it is to change yourself.

Do you know why you don't have what you want? Are you waiting for circumstances to change so you can take advantage of your situation? Circumstances are always changing around us, every minute of every day.

In fact, you should not desire anything in this life except to be in control of your own mind through mastering your thoughts.

What you should be doing is directing this thought energy to work in your favor. You can start to master your focus and concentration by practicing these activities:

Be Aware of Your Distractions

Make a list of these distractions but keep it short. You don't need hundreds of things to think about. My list is less than 10 distractions, which include three major distractions I should be aware of.

Then, when you find yourself suddenly lost or gravitating toward these distractions, you can say, "Okay, I am now focusing on something I had no intention of focusing on."

Awareness of this brings you out of it. By being aware when you fall into the trap of distraction, you can take action to break free. To do this you might have to remove yourself from your environment for a span of time to get refocused. In many cases our distractions are consistently surrounding us.

Remove yourself for just 10 minutes and find a quiet place to think, contemplate, and plan your next hour, if needed. To stay focused, you need to realign your thoughts continuously. It is like a ship on the seas, and this is why the captain is always at the wheel—course correction is an ongoing job. You must be the captain of your own ship and continuously make those slight adjustments to your course.

Read for 30 Minutes a Day

What kind of books do I read? Well, books like the one you are reading right now. I focus on learning the strategies to fully engage my motivation and teach to others how to overcome the fearful thoughts that are keeping them trapped. I read books on setting up and managing an online business platform. If I need a break, I'll switch to fiction for a good story with the hero battling undefeatable odds.

Why is reading important?

Reading keeps you focused in the moment. It improves concentration as studies have shown. Playing games, watching television, or hours spent on social media has the opposite effect. You should reduce your time spent with these activities. It is hard but, the long-term impact is worth more than you could ever know.

Be sure to check at the back of this book when you're done for a complete list of fifty books on my Master Learning list.

Stick to One Task

If you want to really break your concentration and wear out your mind fast, try jumping from task to task. This is multitasking and its effectiveness, or lack of, is a myth.

To be truly effective and maintain your concentration for extended periods of time, stick with one task and work it until it is finished. If this is a big project with multiple tasks, you can do one a day.

If distraction and lack of focus is what fails most people, then the opposite of this is the state of flow. If you really want to explore the endless possibilities of your thinking, and what can be achieved, the state of flow is the way.

What lives in your mind ultimately controls your life.

Ideally, you want to stick to one task until complete. If the task is a project with multiple steps, make sure you complete that step before moving onto anything else. When starting your day, begin by breaking the mold: **Do the one task that is most difficult**.

By getting this out of the way first, it opens the gates for greater flow and increases the energetic flow of creative thoughts. Accomplishing a difficult task before 7 AM should always be the first achievement of the day.

Deep-Breathing Strategy

Breathing has long been a focus for meditation and is a brilliant way to not only reduce stress but improve your ability to concentrate. This is possible because focusing on your breathing is a present-moment action.

We take on average 17,000–30,000 breaths a day. That is a lot of breathing, and most of the time, we aren't thinking about our next breath.

But what happens when you start thinking about your breaths? You become centered, relaxed, and you remove thoughts of worry and fear from your mind.

Deep breathing has immense health benefits, such as:

- Assisting digestion;
- Improving blood circulation to the heart and organs;
- Assisting weight loss;
- Extending your life by reducing stress-induced illnesses; and
- Significantly reducing stress.

So, how do you deep breathe? I'll give you my simple eight-step routine in the morning:

1. Sit comfortably on the floor or in a chair.
2. Begin by breathing normally, focusing on your breaths as you inhale and exhale.
3. Gradually slow down your breathing. Take two to three minutes for this to get into the flow.
4. Next, inhale for a count of four.
5. Hold for a count of four.
6. Exhale for a count of four.
7. Wait for a count of four.
8. Repeat six times.

Chapter 18

Pillar Two:
Unleash the Power of
Strategic Thought

"It's not the situation that's causing your stress, it's your thoughts, and you can change that right here and now. You can choose to be peaceful right here and now. Peace is a choice, and it has nothing to do with what other people do or think."

— Gerald G. Jampolsky, MD

There is no such thing as luck in a successful life. You might get lucky breaks and chalk it up to "being in the right place at the right time"—but something helped put you there. Your success—or lack of it—is a direct result of strategic thought.

What are strategic thoughts and why are they critical?

A journey without a mission becomes the land of confusion. You end up wasting time and energy; two critical resources.

Strategic thought has nothing to do with creating a to-do list or planning your next vacation. It goes deeper than that. If you want to win a war, you have to know the outcome. In other words, you must create the outcome you want. Your thoughts are the building blocks of action.

Strategic thinking means:

- You are executing goals for the long-term;

- You are planning important life events years ahead;

- You are working out complex problems that others can't;

- You are turning vague ideas into concise strategies;

- You are creating long-term plans and goals;

- You are preparing yourself for the unknown; and

- You are connecting with masterminds that discuss and implement plans.

Now, you might be a person who hasn't done much planning in the past. Maybe you winged it, or you lived day-to-day. That works, sometimes—but eventually, you'll have a day when you fail, and you will realize that planning ahead and becoming a strategic planner will clear away the unnecessary obstacles on the path ahead.

This will eliminate distraction and procrastination. It will increase your future potential for greater success in the key areas of your life. You could shift the imbalance in your life right now by deciding to plan an area of your life you've been ignoring.

Don't just plan when you feel like it or wait for the perfect time to get it right. Make strategic thought a necessity in your life. Make it a habit you practice daily. Block off chunks of time every day to plan your next move.

Think deeply about where you want to be—instead of where you think you'll be—based on a mindset of "wait and see."

Throwing chance to the wind is jumping off a cliff and hoping you hit water. That might be a carefree, wild way to live, but if you have a strategy for where you are heading, you will enjoy the trip more without the stress of wondering what is going to happen next.

Here are two areas of your life you can work on right now by applying strategic thought.

Financial Planning

Approximately 78% of Americans are living paycheck to paycheck. One in four have a financial plan. This means a lot of people out there are not thinking about their financial future. This is a great starting point for thinking strategically. Where do you want to be financially in 20 years? 10? Five? How can you create multiple income streams, instead of depending on just one source?

Circumstances play a role in your financial situation, but ultimately, you have the power to change it.

Throw away your excuses. Quit blaming taxes and your employer that doesn't pay you enough. If you struggle with planning this yourself, you can visit an advisor. At the very least, you should educate yourself so that you're not left with nothing in the end.

Here is what I do: At the beginning of the week, I schedule time to think strategically about my financial goals. I review how much I am saving per month, and where I want to be in five years. I review financial goals every week and aim to stay up to date on how progress is being made.

Two books that really helped with strategic planning are *The Automatic Millionaire* by David Bach and *The Total Money Makeover* by Dave Ramsey.

Get serious about your financial plan and apply strategic thought to gaining ground with your cash and assets.

Setting Yearly Goals

Goal planning has always been a struggle for me. I would set out each year with new goals and, by the end of the first quarter end up feeling completely derailed. Why? I was only thinking about the following day, the next week, and beyond that my thoughts would get stuck. So now, I am using Michael Hyatt's *Full Focus Planner* and it has made a massive difference. Instead of just creating a checklist for each day, I was now thinking months ahead, and gradually, planning for the year.

Do you have at least five goals mapped out for this year? If so, how often do you review these goals?

You could be planning for success in just an hour a week. How? I review my goals for the week and month at the beginning of each week. I then think deeply about the action plan for achieving these goals. I have learned that most goals rarely get done by wishing or hoping. You need to be a proactive thinker and make it happen.

Right now, write down five goals for the next three months. Then, take each goal and brainstorm the action steps for each one. Choose the goal that you need to get done first; the goal that is calling to you the most. Make a list of action steps and get to work.

Plan for the Worst / Expect the Best

Someone once told me that you should always be prepared. While we can't predict what is going to happen, we can—at the very least—be ready for it. Be ready for anything. By thinking of all the ways that you can tie up loose ends, you won't be caught in a mess that could have been prevented if you had put in the time to strategically plan for it.

Be aware of when you procrastinate. Procrastinating is a self-defeating habit that can cost you opportunity, money, time, and energy. If this is you, push back against your habit of procrastination. This could be a dominant reason why you have not made bigger plans or accomplished goals. You are afraid to fail. By hanging on to this fear, you fail to move forward.

Think. Plan. Act.

Thoughts by themselves are just ideas, and ideas without follow- up action are just smoke-and-mirrors. Thinking with the intention to build a strategy is the way to go. Push yourself to create the outcome you want. As soon as you have a plan, act on it. Don't wait for that perfect day. People who don't plan and just wait for perfect moments end up having to clean the mess at the end. By then, it's too late.

Chapter 19

Pillar Three:
Apply Creative Thinking and Build an Extraordinary Life

> *"With everything that has happened to you, you can either feel sorry for yourself or treat what has happened as a gift. Everything is either an opportunity to grow or an obstacle to keep you from growing.*
> *You get to choose."*
>
> **— Dr. Wayne W Dyer**

Your imagination is the greatest tool in your mental arsenal. Everything you are creating in your life right now branches from imagination. Imagination leads to ideas, and ideas transform the impossible into a magnificent reality.

We are surrounded by a world built on creative genius. Someone once got famous for saying, "All the good ideas are gone in the world." If that were true, there would be no place for any of us to go. Creativity is very much alive.

Don't hold back your ideas. Let go of the fear of looking silly. Your crazy idea could be the silliest thing that makes people laugh, or the grandest idea of the year. But you'll never know if you don't share your idea with anyone.

Changing, progressing, transitioning, and scaling up require creative level thinking. This doesn't mean you have to be an artist, musician, author, or engineer to be creative. Everyone has a creative genius. The question is, are you thinking with your creative genius, or are you stuck in doing everything the same way because that is the way it has always been done.

Companies that thrive in innovation are immersed in creativity. They expect employees to come up with better methods and systems to improvise, tweak, and, at times, tear down a system that is broken and rebuild it anew.

Here are the questions that creative thinkers ask:

- "What can I do differently today?"
- "How can I improve the quality of my productivity?"
- "What changes could we implement that would be different from anything anyone else is doing?"

Parents raising kids may ask questions like:

- "How can I get my kids to read more books and spend less time on devices?"
- "Where could I take the family for a vacation that would be more enjoyable than Disneyland and much less expensive?"
- "How could I help my child succeed on their next test, so they won't be held back?"

Fix your thoughts on an attitude of having a constant and never-ending improvement mindset. A mindset that is fixed is like locking your ideas away and saying, "I've had enough of creating anything new. I'll just continue to do the same thing over and over again with the same results." This is not a creative attitude, but a destructive one. If you are closed to progress, opportunity and future prospects are lost.

Make it your mission to improve, improvise, and seek that opportunity to make your life better. Make yours better and you make other people's lives better too. Innovation is about building a better tomorrow, a better product, and again, this isn't just in business. You can be innovative at home. You can be creative in everything if you look for ways to boost quality. The winning strategy is this: **Never settle**.

You should never be happy with the way things are, if you really want change to be a part of your life. Never settle for "I've gone as far as I can go," or "This is as good as it gets." It is never finished until you are ready to give up. This is why, when companies restructure, they end up getting rid of many of the employees that have been there for a long time. Sometimes they need a fresh start with new minds that are ready to bring in creative ideas.

Do you know what kills creativity? It isn't a lack of ideas in a project but rather a lack of interest. You can't build an incredible new way of doing something if it is boring. If you're bored or lack interest, you won't work to make it better.

Why do you think most people stop contributing in jobs they hate? They couldn't care less whether the company succeeds or fails. Showing up to a place of employment with the motivation to get a paycheck isn't going to spark your creative imagination. I know because I was immersed in such a job for years. The company had long since lost an environment that fostered creative innovation. The focus was on getting customers (and their money), while using an old system that was obviously breaking down.

The longer I stayed there, the weaker my creativity muscles became. The only way to survive was to quit. Weeks later, working in an environment that stimulated ideas, it was as if I had awakened from the dead. My creative muscles grew by exercising creative thought and challenging myself to come up with new ideas each day.

This brings up a key point. In order to be a prolific creative thinker, surround yourself with a group of people who are focused on building a better world. This can be a mastermind group or a team of creative thinkers. Put yourself in that situation and you will be coming up with ideas and possibilities that you once declared impossible.

Most of today's great inventions we enjoy would never have been born if the inventors had listened to the limiting beliefs of critics and cynics. Someone will always be there to tell you "That is impossible." But what they really mean is it's impossible for them, not you.

My best suggestion: Cut that tie and move on. Be the one who takes that chance and tries something different. Be okay with failing at it, learning from your mistakes, and doing it better on your next attempt.

Here are a few ideas to get you started on thinking creatively. Ask yourself how you would answer these questions.

- "How can I double my monthly income in the next six months?"
- "How can I help someone lose 20 pounds without dieting?"
- "How can we reduce the amount of time employees are spending on email by 50%?"
- "How can I boost self-confidence in my kids, so they will become unstoppable, fear-busting human beings?"
- "How can I reduce the amount of our bills by half?"
- "How can I make eating at home interesting by introducing new recipes to my family?"

> *"The only place where your dream becomes impossible is in your own thinking."*
>
> **— Robert H Schuller**

Questions are the answer. Whenever you need to improve an area of your life that is stuck, begin to brainstorm the possibilities. Make notes and record your ideas. Then, take the best of those ideas and try them out. Test your idea before throwing it out. But don't give up after the first couple of failures. Give your ideas a chance. Sometimes, they just need a push.

Continue to ask yourself, "How can I improve this?" Nothing is ever finished. We can always do better, create better, and apply better ideas to creating or improving a system so that it functions like a well-oiled machine.

Here are seven reasons why you should be a creative thinker and spark that imagination to work:

Creative Thinking Triggers Big Questions

Big thinkers ask the right questions. If you think big you are ready to challenge the ideas and old beliefs of everyone else. You may not be the most popular person in the room, but you could be the smartest person. People will look to you for leadership and direction, not because your ideas are the best, but because you have the courage to voice your creative vision.

Creative Thinking Builds Bridges

Your thoughts are like bridges that carry you from Point A to Point Z. By applying your thoughts and harnessing that energy to work toward better developments, you can see the bridges of creation take hold. This attracts better opportunity and bridges the gap between clarity and confusion.

Creative Thinking Taps into Impossible Possibilities

Believe it is possible, and it is. Be a nonbeliever, and nothing becomes possible. What is possible and what isn't is largely based on perspective. By working on ideas that are radical or "out there", the possibilities become more real.

You can turn your world into something that you only ever imagined. Remove the negative thoughts from your mind that say, "It's been all done before," or "They tried that, and it didn't work."

Creative Thinkers Celebrate Freedom

There is great freedom in being creative. You can set your own pace and stop relying on others to give you the answers. Seek your own solutions and feel alive because you are working toward a freedom that you can create and own.

Creative thinking puts you in the **captain's seat of life.** You feel in control of your destiny when your imagination is allowed to explore and do what it does best: Create. Let your thoughts go and recognize when they try to hold you back.

Creative Thinking Builds an Extraordinary Life

Need proof? I can drop a hundred names in here right now of creative people who have built empires from nothing but their imagination. We don't have space for a thousand names, so how about 10? See any names you recognize? Can you add to the list?

- Steven Spielberg
- Jim Henson
- JK Rowling
- Charles Ives
- John Williams
- Walt Disney
- Benjamin Franklin
- George Lucas
- William Shakespeare
- Thomas Edison

You can build that extraordinary life you are imagining. Anything becomes possible the moment we remove doubt and replace it with opportunity. Create your own opportunity by creating your own thing, and then work for it to make it yours.

Creative Thinking Kills Fear and Uncertainty

Being a creative thinker puts you in charge of your own destiny. This is a huge win when it comes to removing fearful thoughts from your mind. In fact, fear and creativity cannot exist together. When you take these creative thoughts and apply action, you remove all fear. Action destroys fear. It doesn't matter if you succeed or not. What matters is you are doing something and trying to forge ahead.

Uncertainty spreads when indecision is present. When not feeling sure of ourselves or stuck because of the fear to move ahead, then you get caught up in the fear of "What if I try and fail? What if this idea doesn't succeed? What if I don't make it and I have to face all those people?"

Be a person of action. Say no to the fear that keeps your mind trapped. Be bigger than your doubt. Let your creative juices pour out of you. Say yes to everything that is opening up before you.

Creative Thinkers are Happy People

Expressing creativity releases endorphins in the brain and this is like swallowing a happy pill. Do you ever notice when you are working on something creative, you just naturally feel good? There is a good reason for this.

Human beings are born as creative creatures. We can't *not* be thinking about something. Unfortunately, many people don't use their thinking in creative ways. Rather, they think about bad things that happened. They get hung up on failures of the past and old resentments. This destroys creativity and replaces it with misery.

I write books, as you know. Do I do this for loads of cash and to become a famous author? Well, while I can make a living at it and have become well-known and gained some fame, writing makes me feel good. I know what I create is having an impact on people, and if this book or— the many others I have published—has an impact, then creativity is working miracles through my craft.

Chapter 20

Pillar Four:
Destroy Fear With
Confident Action

*"Happiness is an attitude. We either make ourselves
miserable, or happy and strong.
The amount of work is the same."*

— Francesca Reigler

Until acted upon, every thought is just an idea. Many of these ideas are good. A few are great. But it takes more than a great idea to change the world. You need to act on your thoughts to turn your creativity into a reality.

Have you ever heard someone tell you about all the ideas they said they were going to act on but never did? Or all the plans they had made that never went anywhere?

Anyone can come up with an idea. But the few will act on it. Why? Several reasons. First, we are creatures of fear. Before we make a move, our mind is already coming up with a dozen reasons why we shouldn't. Then you abandon that good idea and come up with another one. You sit on that for a while and the cycle repeats itself. So, to push forward and transform thought into reality, action is needed.

Here are three steps to turn good ideas into tangible action steps.

Start with a Small Action Step

If you are thinking about cleaning up your home and you don't know where to start, begin with a small step. Pick something up off the floor. Do it again. Soon, you will build up more motivation to keep going. This is momentum building for breaking procrastination.

Begin Your Morning Doing the Most Difficult task First

I'll admit that I am a sucker for doing what it easy first. I could do this all day. But this builds a lazy habit of doing a bunch of easy tasks that don't add up to real progress. Your first thought of the day should be, "What one task am I putting off that I could do first?" I say, get it done first. You'll feel great for the rest of the day. Thinking about doing it won't get it done. It will just build more excuses.

Reduce the Amount of Times You Say, "I'll Think About It."

Another habit of mine, that initially leads to further procrastination, is saying, "I'll think about it." After I say these words, I actually stop thinking about it altogether. I realized that I had turned this expression into an open door to put something off, especially if I didn't want to deal with it at that time.

In fact, I rarely wanted to deal with most things in the moment. So, before you say, "I'll think about it", ask yourself, "Is this an action that I can take right now? Can I do this thing now? Is there a good reason why I should do this later as opposed to now?"

Be aware of when you use this expression to put something off. If there is anything that can be done right now, do it right now. In fact, my new motto is "Do It Now." I don't wait. If I do, it just gets put on the back burner. What I discovered is that my back burner was full of old tasks that had been shoved back there for many years.

Take massive action and make it your first action step of the day. There is a time to plan for things, yes, but most action plans begin before every detail is decided. You do have to start with something. There is always something that you can start with. Don't be that person who is still making excuses years later and keeps talking about doing the same things that ultimately never get done.

Stay focused on destroying your fear before it ruins you. Don't let fear win. Push back. Hard. If you let lazy mental habits have their way, you'll be left with a closet full of empty promises and half-finished projects that take up your space and stick with you. Your mind will hold onto the tasks it hasn't finished. Open loops use up mental energy when we have to continuously think about them.

The key to this is to close your loops. At the end of each day, I identify the tasks I didn't get done. Then, I move these tasks to the next day and make sure they are first on my list in the morning. I do the hard tasks first because I am most likely to procrastinate on them.

Confident Action Creates Confident Thinking

If you allow yourself to procrastinate on the things you know require your attention, this will kill your confidence. You see, your confidence meter is like a bank. When you make deposits that are actionable, you are stocking up on confidence. Soon you are rich with confidence because of all the deposits you have made.

The reverse is also true. Procrastinate and ignore the work that needs to be done and you are reducing your confidence bank. We refer to confident thinking as if it should come first, but actually, when you act, you shift your thoughts to be more positive. In other words, confident action builds confident thought. If you need proof, try it out.

Do something right now that you've been putting off. Is there an application you haven't filled out yet? Is your house a mess? Has your homework been left undone? Are your taxes still not filed, and the deadline is this week?

I challenge you right now to do one thing that is waiting on your to-do list that you've been ignoring. Procrastinating affects us all in a negative way. You feed yourself negative thoughts with abrasive words that sound like this:

- "You are so lazy."

- "How long has this been going on?"

- "Everyone else is succeeding; why aren't you?"

174 · SCOTT ALLAN

Confident action. Confident speech. Confident thoughts. These three elements are interconnected to make you an unstoppable force. Confidence isn't something you build up one day and let go of the next. You have to keep at it by doing something every day that continues to add to your confidence bank. As soon as you stop acting, the negativity looks for a way to slip back into your life. You have to guard your mind at all times.

Positive action is how you defeats your fears. You have to think about the actions that are right, and then take those actions. Remember, as I said before (and will reinforce here), fear is destroyed when you move forward with the right thoughts and actions.

I have never met a fearful person who was full of energy and had a positive outlook on life. Physical action is the precursor to a positive lifestyle. Forward motion creates positive emotion.

Here is a list of positive actions that will change your attitude and perspective:

- Walk with your eyes up and pick up your speed.

- Only say good things about people even if you have a gripe against them.

- Greet everyone you meet with an enthusiastic smile and say, "It's great to know you."

- Remove thoughts of greed and malice—two very damaging thought patterns.

- Think of five ways you can help someone today.

- Manage your anger even when someone else is lashing out.

- Stay in control of your emotions.

Guard Your Mind Against
Evil Forces

"We will be more successful in all our endeavors if we can let go of the habit of running all the time, and take little pauses to relax and re-center ourselves. And we'll also have a lot more joy in living."

— Thich Nhat Hanh

Of the 35+ books I've published to date, *Empower Your Thoughts* has been one of my favorite books. It is amazing to watch the transformation that happens in a person's life when they shift their way of thinking.

I've seen people change relationships, move to places they never dreamed, and take charge of a life that at one time appeared hopeless and futile.

When you make a shift in your mindset, your thought patterns open up and you create a positive funnel for lasting change.

In a book that I read as part of my morning routine, *The Teaching of Buddha* by the **Bukkyo Dendo Kyokai**, there is a passage that states:

"Human beings tend to move in the direction of their thoughts. If they harbor greedy thoughts, they become more greedy; if they

think angry thoughts, they become more angry; if they hold foolish thoughts, their feet move in that direction."

Your thoughts direct action, and it is your action that drives your destiny. But the word "action" doesn't have to apply to doing something.

Meditation is an action—even if you are sitting still for a length of time. The act of meditation is practicing mind mastery, and without having control of your mind, all the actions you take will likely be haphazard, disorganized steps in the wrong direction.

Focusing in on your thoughts is an action, too. It is an action of the mind as you direct energy toward making the thoughts that harbor positivity.

This is why your life will always move in the direction of your thoughts.

A mind that is well-guarded against the enemies of bad thinking can hold its own under the worst of conditions. There are many times in a given day when your mind will be put to the test: by people you are surrounded with for 8-10 hours in an office, family and friends, or unseen obstacles appearing out of nowhere attempting to derail you.

There are days of peace when nothing could go wrong, and days of chaos when it is all wrong. But regardless the state of the world, your spouse's temper tantrum, or the state of unfavorable conditions, you have total control over how you react to everything.

It is never the circumstances that make us anxious, angry, or lose power; it is only our perception of these circumstances and how we choose to act in the moment.

Will you get angry? Resentful? Wish that none of this was happening to you? Although your mind may be at peace, everything around you—including the chaos of people—is in turmoil.

People surrounding you are restless, irritable, greedy, needy, wanting, craving. When under the influence of environment, we seek to escape. You might run or avoid people to stay away from being pulled into the chaos of drama.

But what we escape from is left unattended. You can't leave a garden unattended just because it has been taken over by weeds and insects. You set up another garden, and the same thing happens again.

What if you run into the house and they follow you? Will you abandon your home? So, you leave your home and escape into another town, only to find that they have the same bug problem.

A master of the mind can walk into any situation and become the pillar that remains unbroken. They can do this because they have trained the mind to stay true and focused.

Mind control is about mind mastery and being able to filter out the bad thoughts that lead to misdirected action. As long as your mind is under control, you don't have to worry about being taken over by the lesser desires that are constantly looking for a way in.

You are the master of your thoughts, the Warrior of Your Own Mind, and the guardian at the gate of your conscious mind.

Stay fixed on the path of freedom—The freedom to choose your own mind, to avoid delusion, and to stop clinging to situations that make empty promises.

Your mind is the true master, and you are the grand artist of your thoughts.

Keep on dreamin'.

Scott Allan

"Whatever you habitually think yourself to be, that you are. You must form, now, a greater and better habit; you must form a conception of yourself as a being of limitless power, and habitually think that you are that being. It is the habitual, not the periodical thought that decides your destiny."

—Wallace D. Wattle

About Scott Allan

Scott Allan is an international bestselling author of over 30 books published in 12 languages in the area of personal growth and self-development. He is the author of **Fail Big**, **Undefeated,** and **Do the Hard Things First**.

As a former corporate business trainer in Japan, and **Transformational Mindset Strategist**, Scott has invested over 10,000 hours of research and instructional coaching into the areas of self-mastery and leadership training.

With an unrelenting passion for teaching, building critical life skills, and inspiring people around the world to take charge of their lives, Scott Allan is committed to a path of **constant and never-ending self-improvement**.

Many of the success strategies and self-empowerment material that is reinventing lives around the world evolves from Scott Allan's 20 years of practice and teaching critical skills to corporate executives, individuals, and business owners.

You can connect with Scott at:

scottallan@scottallanpublishing.com

www.scottallanpublishing.com

www.scottallanbooks.com

Scott Allan

Master Your Life One Book at a Time.

PATHWAYS

TO

BY SCOTT ALLAN

MASTERY

THE SERIES

Made in United States
Troutdale, OR
05/18/2024